P9-CRB-190

Merry Christmas
to Anne

from Dad that 1988

Silverware

Alain Gruber

Silverware

RIZZOLI
NEW YORK

To Margaret and Werner Abegg

French language edition, L'Argenterie de maison
du XVIe au XIXe siècle
© 1982 by Office du Livre
English translation by David Smith

© 1982 by Office du Livre
First published in the United States of America in 1982 by

*R*IZZOLI INTERNATIONAL PUBLICATIONS, INC.
712 Fifth Avenue/New York 10019

All rights reserved
No part of this book may be reproduced in any manner whatsoever
without permission of Rizzoli International Publications, Inc.

Library of Congress Cataloging in Publication Data

Gruber, Alain Charles.
   Silverware.
   Translation of: L'Argenterie de maison.
   1. Silverware–History. I. Title.
NK7106.G7813 1982   739.2′383   82-50422
ISBN 0-8478-0440-2

Printed and bound in Switzerland

Table of Contents

Introduction

I have been given such freedom in my choice of illustrations for this book that I have had recourse not only to the plans of specialists in decorative themes and to silversmiths' models, but also to reproductions of silver objects. This fair distribution is, in my opinion, essential to a proper understanding of the objects produced for domestic use by silversmiths between the sixteenth and the nineteenth centuries. If we were to confine ourselves merely to those works that have almost miraculously survived, our view would of necessity be very incomplete, since it would omit all the silverware planned but never produced throughout those four centuries.

The survival of the silversmith's work is constantly threatened. Silver objects are far more likely to be destroyed than, for example, furniture, paintings, ceramics or glassware. Silver is a very valuable commodity and can always be used again for other purposes. For this reason individuals have never hesitated to sacrifice the silverware of an earlier age and have melted down precious objects whenever financial necessity has compelled them to do so. Not only individuals but states, too, have shown again and again that they are quite ready to destroy works of art made of precious materials such as gold and silver when the economic need has arisen. Both the rich treasures of silver-plate owned by monarchs and the more modest collections of private individuals have often been melted down as the direct consequence of sumptuary laws.

Church silver, on the other hand, has frequently escaped destruction, mainly because of the widespread respect felt for objects that had a sacred function. This, of course, is one of the principal reasons why religious objects made of silver have, at certain periods of history and in certain places at least, been preserved in a much better state and in far greater numbers than those made for civil use.

Silverware, then, has been officially melted down in one unhappy period of history after another, with the rise and fall of the fortunes of individuals and states. There has, however, also been another reason for its disappearance. Changes in artistic taste, the decline of certain customs and practices and the transformation of social habits and even of the whole way of life have often led to the apparently arbitrary, and therefore unforgivable, but none the less understandable decision to destroy silver works of art. Specialists who have studied this problem have come to the conclusion that silversmiths who were entrusted with the task of making out-of-date silverware in the eighteenth century in fact destroyed as many pieces as they created! This practice was, moreover, very widespread at a time when the cost of labour was minimal in comparison with that of the material itself and when it was as common to change one's silver-plate as it was to change one's furniture or any other work produced by craftsmen that was especially subject to variations in fashion.

The destruction of silver objects is, of course, very much to be regretted in itself, but the pattern has been different from country to country. It has depended on the changing political, economic and artistic fortunes of each society. This accounts for the gaps in the heritage of silverware found in every part of Europe. In America a considerable number of silver objects have been preserved, since the European tradition in art and craftsmanship has been nurtured more carefully than in Europe.

An immense amount of silverware has been lost in France, and particularly in its artistic centre, Paris. Many of these articles were lost in wars or because governments forced Frenchmen to have their silver melted down at times of economic crisis. However, another and even more heart-breaking phenomenon has been especially evident in French history: nowhere else in Europe have radical changes in taste led to so many instances of often well-intentioned destruction of silver objects from generation to generation. This is one very good reason why a consideration merely of those pieces of silverware that have miraculously survived every threat of destruction cannot provide a sufficient basis nowadays to illustrate the extremely wide range of silverware—both plentiful and brilliant on the one hand and both carefully prepared and inventive on the other—that was designed or produced in France. French silversmiths' work had an influence of incalculable importance on every country in Europe.

During the sixteenth century Spain and Portugal were able to make use of precious metals which they obtained very cheaply in their American colonies, with the result that this was a very productive period in the Iberian peninsula. The cost of silver fell fourteen times in less than a hundred years. Despite this great wealth, it was the Church rather than the Habsburg and Bourbon rulers of Spain that took advantage of this situation in order to fill the treasures of its sanctuaries with splendid, heavy and finely wrought gold and silverware. The Spanish court was noted more for the refinement of its ceremonial than for outstanding artistic merit. The country as a whole also rapidly became poorer and this did not encourage silversmiths to produce a great number of civil objects. Until a taste for French silver became widespread in Spain in the eighteenth century, there were relatively few pieces and these were simple in form and imposing rather than elegant in style.

Until the seventeenth century Flanders and the Low Countries exercised an obvious influence on Spanish silversmiths. Portugal, on the other hand, was oriented towards England, as far as its silver was concerned, although the royal family had magnificent silver imported from Paris in the eighteenth century. Nowadays Lisbon—together with Leningrad, New York and Buenos Aires—is one of the leading centres of the eighteenth-century Parisian silversmith's craft.

The silversmiths of Antwerp not only played a particularly important part in the development of Spanish silverware in the sixteenth and seventeenth centuries, but also had a considerable influence on the rest of Europe. Flanders and the Low Countries were both extremely rich in these two centuries and were therefore able to produce silver objects of a very high quality.

By the end of the sixteenth century, Antwerp silversmiths in particular were producing magnificent silver. Fit for a king, it was based on a very original recasting of ideas borrowed either directly from Italy or by way of the Italianate schools of Fontainebleau and Paris. From the eighteenth century onwards they developed a style that was marked by many different influences. A number of very great artists emerged at that time whose names have since been regarded as among the greatest in the European silver industry.

Although Italy continued to excel in every sphere of artistic production, both in the number of works and in their high quality, from the sixteenth century onwards, it produced relatively little silver for civil use. One clear reason for this very modest interest was that the country had no colonies yielding a plentiful supply of precious metals. The artists of the towns on the Italian peninsula all preferred to work with lighter, more cheerful and less expensive materials. The desire for change and illusion always seemed to predominate over the need to invest in valuable and therefore often cripplingly costly materials. The Church in Italy, like the Spanish Church, was also brilliantly triumphant in the Baroque age and accumulated much of the gold and silver that was available at the time. Finally, almost all the civil gold and silver plate that was left in Italy at the end of the eighteenth century fell into the hands of the revolutionary French armies that laid the country waste.

The situation was radically different in England. As an island, it did not suffer from invasions and the silver that disappeared over the centuries was destroyed by Englishmen themselves during civil disturbances. A great number of silver pieces of English origin can be traced back to the sixteenth and especially to the seventeenth and eighteenth centuries. This can also be explained by the traditional taste for silver in England. The English very soon became enthusiastic collectors of early objects of artistic value. This protected early gold- and silverware from being destroyed, in the way that it so often was on the Continent, as a result of changes in taste.

The German-speaking people have also produced and collected a great deal of silverware throughout the centuries. Although their countries have also frequently been laid waste by terrible wars, their innate respect for the silversmith's work has resulted in many pieces being saved from destruction. The extremely powerful merchant guilds in these countries accumulated treasures of inestimable value and have often continued to add to them. The greatest losses occurred during the wars at the end of the eighteenth and the beginning of the nineteenth centuries.

In the Scandinavian and Slav countries silver objects for civil use were for the most part produced much later than in other European nations. Although at times these articles have been made in fairly large quantities, they have certainly been fewer in number and have always lacked originality. German, English and French silver articles have been imported in great numbers.

This is an extremely brief survey of the reasons why so much European silver has been lost or destroyed. I have provided it mainly in order to justify my decision to refer again and again throughout this book to engravings, paintings and other illustrations of meals and tables set with silverware. Many of these are naive and others real works of art, but they can all help us to form a more complete picture of the silverware that was designed and sometimes made for civil use between the sixteenth and the nineteenth centuries.

The fact that so many silver objects have been lost or melted down also accounts for our persistently wrong assessment of those objects. It must be borne in mind that they were created for a definite purpose and a precise function. That function is often completely forgotten or overlooked nowadays. It is true, of course, that the isolation in which many precious examples of the silversmith's craft are kept allows the inherent qualities of these articles to be more easily evaluated by both the specialist and the amateur. At the same time, however, this isolation from the objects' original context also results in a false interpretation. That is why I have tried to put the works considered in this volume back into their original and natural environment. In the first part of this book I have attempted to recreate the historical framework in which they were used and displayed in the houses and palaces of our ancestors.

The contemporary illustrations that I have taken from various countries and different periods are full of instructions and descriptions. These may at first sight seem tedious, but they can help us to appreciate more fully the many details that are depicted. It is very regrettable that this obvious desire to enable later generations to gain a clear insight into so many aspects and details of the history of European silver from the sixteenth to the nineteenth century in its original setting was not shared with equal enthusiasm in all the countries where such objects were produced. Although my choice of these illustrations is of necessity very restricted, it does, I think, provide a sufficient basis for the historical development of the silversmith's work in Europe to be retraced.

In the second part of this book I have attempted to give a typological outline of the most important silver articles used in the house. I have dealt with these articles mainly from the point of view of their practical use at table, and have considered them not only as decorative pieces on the table, but also in their employment in everyday life. What emerges very clearly from this study is that our ancestors were far less exact than has often been suggested about the function they assigned to these objects. Their precise purpose cannot always be defined with absolute certainty. Before the nineteenth century no one would have dreamed of limiting an article to one exclusive use.

The same applies to the terminology employed. This was always vague and imprecise—even in that work which has such a high reputation for precision and minute detail, the monumental eighteenth-century *Encyclopaedia* of Diderot and d'Alembert. We have therefore chosen the most simple and classical terms in order to describe as clearly as possible the use that the silversmiths intended for the objects they created.

Finally, I do not claim to provide the reader with an exhaustive catalogue of all the silver objects ever listed. There are very many excellent books specializing in the silver of the different European countries and America which provide a much more precise answer than I can give here to the questions asked by the ever increasing number of collectors of early silverware.

Part I
The Silver Sideboard

In the Middle Ages civil and domestic silverware was regarded as too valuable simply to be arranged on the table. All table silver was therefore placed, together with other utensils that were to be used throughout the meal, on a piece of furniture specially designed for this purpose—a dresser, sideboard or console table. We need not spend much time considering the earliest examples of this type of furniture. All that needs to be said is that they were originally like the tables at which the meals themselves were eaten: that is, they were set up temporarily in the rooms or halls where the meals were served. In great houses a cup-bearer would stand at one of the dressers preparing and mixing the drinks that he was later to serve at table. Certain dishes which had been brought from the kitchens, which were often at a considerable distance from the dining-hall, would also be arranged on these dressers. The food would be kept warm there, prepared, cut up and above all 'tested' to prevent any attempt to poison a guest. The household staff responsible for this task also had to guard and care for the silver treasures that were kept on the dressers.

From the end of the Middle Ages onwards silver became increasingly common in the courts of Europe, with the result that a special kind of dresser was evolved and used in the more magnificent of these courts, above all in Italy. These dressers were built in several tiers, on which the pieces of silverware to be used at table were displayed. The design of these sideboards may have been based on church altars. What is certain is that these shelved pieces of furniture with their valuable and beautiful contents were very decorative and ostentatious.

During the Baroque period the design of these dressers and the number of shelves they could contain were strictly laid down according to the position which the noble family possessing the silver occupied in the clearly defined class hierarchy. The dressers therefore gradually lost their utilitarian function and became more and more emphatically a means for displaying wealth. Increasing attention was devoted to filling them with objects which could never have been used at table but were clearly there to be seen and admired. They contained extremely precious pieces of silver; some of these were so old that they had become too fragile to use and others had fallen out of fashion, but all had ceased to have any function.

When did these sideboards containing silver objects made for the most part simply as showpieces originate? It is impossible to determine this exactly. Early examples were certainly in use at the end of the Middle Ages, at the courts of the Valois, the dukes of Burgundy and the Emperor and the homes of wealthy Italian aristocrats.

Among several examples of Italian sideboards going back to the Mannerist period, one of the most characteristic and least known can be seen in the mural paintings by Giulio Romano (1492-1546) in the Palazzo del Te at Mantua (c. 1525). It was undoubtedly copied by the artist from a model that existed. The buffet in the hall of *Love and Psyche* is still very much admired. It is especially interesting because we can learn a great deal from it about early sixteenth-century silverware and the use to which silver was put in decorating such pieces of furniture. It is basically a table, covered with a white cloth reaching down to the floor. At the back are two tiers of shelves. The painter has filled this buffet with a mixture of objects, some of them taken from earlier written sources or illustrations.

The reproductions of early silverware featured in this painting are all the more valuable in view of the fact that hardly any of the silver objects which were made at this time and which had such a decisive influence on later products, have survived. It is, for example, possible to distinguish, behind several bowls with two handles, a set of silver plates which can be included among the earliest prototypes of plates that are found quite frequently a century later. These plates are based on a type that is well known to us in porcelain models. They have very wide rims and bodies which are heavily embossed and are very similar in shape to soup-bowls.

1 *The Hall of Love and Psyche*, showing the great silver sideboard. Detail of fresco ▷ by Giulio Romano (1492-1546) in the Palazzo del Te, Mantua, c. 1525.

2 Banqueting-hall in Mary of Hungary's palace at Binche, showing three tables placed one above the other and the surrounding decoration. The feast was held in 1549 in honour of King Philip II of Spain. Anonymous drawing. Bibliothèque Royale Albert Ier, Brussels.

3 Design for a silver sideboard by Domenico Bolognese, Bologna, late 17th century. Cooper-Hewitt Museum, New York. 1938-88-2596.

On the first shelf is an interesting silver-gilt salt, at that time the most important decorative piece of silver on the table. The salt container itself is pyramidal in shape. A fine leather-covered canteen containing a dozen little knives, known at the time as *parepains*, can also be seen.

The most striking articles illustrated on the upper shelf are two delicate and partly gilded ewers with basins, a silver jug, and a very curious pouring-vessel made of silver, partly gilded and shaped like a duck. The latter is clearly a precursor of those hanaps in animal form that were so popular in sixteenth-century Germany. It also in a sense foreshadows those remarkable porcelain illusions so common in the eighteenth century. A silver, flask-shaped flagon can also be seen, resting in a great wine-cooler. The whole painting illustrates the great quantity and variety of silverware that existed during the Mannerist period. In their shapes these silver objects anticipate the monumental pieces that were produced in the Baroque age.

A curious and clumsy northern European imitation of these Italian tiered silver sideboards was made for a ceremony arranged by Mary of Hungary in her palace at Binche in 1549 in recognition of King Philip II of Spain. This 'dresser' consists basically of three

4　Design for a silver buffet by Henry de Gissey for the pavilion erected in the park of the Palace of Versailles for the feasts of 1668. Kunstbibliothek, Berlin (Staatliche Museen Preussischer Kulturbesitz). Hdz 109.

tables of equal size one above the other, each containing many silver objects. They are covered by a monumental canopy supported by four columns and the entire extraordinary structure is illuminated by an arrangement of lamps. The fantastic decoration is full of political allusions of the kind that were so popular at the time. The silver articles displayed on the three tables are typically mid-sixteenth-century: covered hanaps, cups with stems, mugs, salts, pouring-vessels and table-fountains.

The whole structure and display is decorated with human and animal statuettes. It is based on an Italian model. The upper table has a centrepiece in the form of an allegorical tree which serves as an embellishment for the sweet and savoury items taken between the main courses. Despite the fact that the tables can be brought down mechanically to the level of the guests, what this buffet, with its tier upon tier of elaborate silverware, achieves above all is a studied decorative effect. The mechanism also looks forward to the reign of Louis XV of France, when moving tables so delighted the guests at Choisy and Trianon.

Many engravings and paintings show French, Italian or German silver sideboards in the seventeenth century, since this was the great period of this type of furniture. Their display consists for the most part of a careful selection of pieces chosen for their attractive appearance together with other, more humble articles that were clearly used at table.

The most magnificent and varied illustrations of silver displayed on buffets are undoubtedly those which were prepared by Italian artists and commissioned by a special court department at the Palace of Versailles known as the 'Petty Pleasures'. These artists made very careful engravings of the silver shown or used at the great feasts given by the young Louis XIV at the palace and the sideboards on which it was displayed. The memory of these displays was perpetuated by these illustrations, and the courts of Europe were inspired by them. There can be no doubt that they helped to set the tone in ostentatious silverware elsewhere in Europe. These engravings are unfortunately the only evidence that remains of the enormous collection of domestic silverware at Versailles. All the palace silver disappeared very soon after it had been produced when events forced the king to have it melted down.

Versailles was the great centre in Europe of the art of the silver sideboard in the second half of the eighteenth century. It was there that this way of displaying silverware reached its climax. These sideboards were designed for the feasts that took place year after year in the palace and its park. They reflect the unlimited imagination of the great artists employed by the French kings. These works were so brilliant that they inspired the palace architects and gardeners, who imitated the most successful side-boards and their silver displays in various constructions, fountains and works on the estate. The stepped waterfall in the ballroom, the fountain of the pyramid at the end of the turnip-bed and the water sideboard in the garden of Trianon are good examples of this.

In the seventeenth and eighteenth centuries silver sideboards were not used simply for their decorative effect in banqueting-halls. Almost everywhere in Europe they also had a special place at banquets held in gardens. There are monumental examples of their employment in an open-air setting in Italy, France, Germany and the Low Countries.

A particularly fine buffet covered with very interesting pieces of silver is illustrated in a painting of a rustic banquet by Esaias van de Velde. It is hardly surprising that there were many such paintings by artists in the Netherlands, since there had long been an interest in nature in that country. In this picture the step-like shelves are placed at the back of and above a table draped with a costly

5   A table and a silver sideboard erected for a feast held in Bologna in 1693. Print by Giacomo Giovanini, based on Marcantonio Chiarini. Biblioteca comunale dell'Archiginnasio, Bologna.

6   A rustic banquet with a silver sideboard. Detail of a picture by Esaias van de Velde (*c.* 1591-1630), Netherlands, *c.* 1600. Private collection.

7   Banquet held in honour of the Empress Maria Teresa of Austria at Vienna in 1740. *Foreground*: senior public servants are seated around a richly adorned table; *background, left*: a great silver sideboard; *right*: a sideboard for drinks. Anonymous print.

17

table-cover, which is in turn protected by a damask linen cloth descending like a cascade from the uppermost step. The steps themselves are full of beautiful silver objects that have obviously been placed on this sideboard either for their decorative effect or else to be used during a meal at the table in the background. Assembled around a magnificent pie in the shape of a bird are many objects designed in accordance with the prevalent Flemish taste in silverware. They include a drum-shaped salt with ball feet, a hanap in the form of a bunch of grapes, three romer cups set on great and elaborate silver stands, two cups or tazzas, as they were known in Italy, a very large hanap, a nautilus cup and several spoons mixed with various glasses of the kind fashionable in the Netherlands in the early seventeenth century.

The leading cabinet-makers in Europe from the sixteenth century onwards worked in Germany, making most of the astonishing sideboards on which private individuals permanently exhibited their silver treasures. Many articles were especially made for such exhibitions, and indeed the existence of certain sets of silverware cannot be satisfactorily explained apart from their arrangement and display on sideboards. The prosperous guilds of merchants and tradesmen in the German and Swiss towns of the period kept treasures of gold and silverware which were to some extent at least the outward sign of their wealth. A candidate seeking membership of one of these guilds was often asked to set the seal on his admission by giving a valuable silver object to the association or else by contributing to the purchase of a particularly large and costly article. In this way guilds built up collections of incalculable value, which often took the place of purely monetary reserves. Despite the inevitable losses that occurred during wars and revolutions, many of these treasures are still in existence, at least in part, in the keeping of the societies and associations that have to a great extent replaced the original guilds. The astonishing hanaps, created in such extraordinary and improbable shapes in the seventeenth century, can perhaps be explained in the light of these merchant guilds. Many heraldic and even political pretexts of a purely allegorical kind led to the invention of silverware pieces in which the maker's imagination seems to have run wild.

An eighteenth-century buffet that was worthy to hold and display guild treasures is illustrated in an engraving of a banquet organized in 1740 in honour of Maria Teresa of Austria. There are in fact two such sideboards in the background of this picture, one on each side of the main entrance to the banqueting-hall. The more important of the two sideboards contains about fifty pieces of silver, many of them quite remarkable. Among the most prominent objects are two great wine-coolers, several immense dishes, piles of

8 The great silver-gilt buffet or console table in the Hall of Knights in the Royal Palace of Berlin, 1703. Print by Martin Engelbrecht (1684-1756), based on Eosander de Göthe. Private collection.

9 A great silver sideboard. Still life by Alexandre François Desportes, Paris, c. ▷ 1720. Metropolitan Museum of Art, New York. (Purchased from Bequest of Mary Wetmore Shively in Memory of her Husband, Henry L. Shively, M.D., 1964.) 64.315.

plates, a set of goblets, a large canteen containing a set of knives, forks and spoons and a centrepiece consisting of a coffee- or tea-service with drinking bowls, a sugar-dish and spoons arranged in the form of a crown. Artistic taste was often very conservative in German-speaking countries. This accounts for the presence of very out-of-date hanaps, dating back to the seventeenth century or even earlier, alongside more modern objects. On each side of these buffets are more modest dressers, used for serving drinks. They are full of flagons of brandy and bottles of wine; the servants go to them to refill the glasses of the guests as the latter call for more to drink. The dining-table itself is lavishly decorated and provided with countless dishes of every kind.

The gigantic buffet erected in 1703 against one wall of the Hall of Knights in the Royal Palace in Berlin is a classical model of the sideboard for displaying showpieces. Only very costly, luxurious articles can be seen at different levels in the illustration of it. It is surmounted by a monumental canopy, below which are many little consoles, arranged on the wall for the sole purpose of impressing visitors. It was not built to accommodate a great number of articles in everyday use that were to be displayed on one occasion only. The perfectly symmetrical arrangement of the pieces illustrated and their exceptionally fine quality point clearly to a permanent exhibition. Two very large fountains or cisterns with their basins are prominently featured, one at each extremity of the large console at the lowest level. They are very reminiscent of the silver furnishings at Versailles or the monumental pieces of silverware made for guilds in England at that time.

The few surviving examples of these objects bear witness to the luxurious nature of such enormous pieces. In the middle of the bottom console here is a fountain of more modest design and dimensions, with a cooler for wine-glasses on each side. The space between this main level at the base and the top of the dresser is filled with nine identical ewers with basins and eight silver flasks. At the top of the structure is a great dish adorned with figures. This acts as a link between the buffet itself and its splendid canopy. Such vast sideboards must have had a profound decorative effect. There was also another, more practical reason for displaying silver in this way. The many brilliant silver objects also acted as reflectors, increasing the amount of light in the halls where they were exhibited.

Silver articles can be combined with other objects made of much lighter substances more effectively than in any other way on these French buffets, or on sideboards based on French models at the beginning of the eighteenth century. The results, known to us from paintings of the period, are often colourful and very pleasing. Flowers and various kinds of food, especially fruit, were brought together with the most magnificent pieces of table silverware. Several of Desportes's pictures featuring these sideboards are excellent still-life compositions. A fine example of his work is in the Metropolitan Museum of New York. It depicts a marble buffet adorned with silver pieces arranged in perfect symmetry. At the lowest level is a centrepiece consisting of a round silver salver with a convoluted rim, and two fauns on the base. A bowl of fruit is situated between these fauns, which support on their backs one of those famous pyramids of food of various kinds which were so highly valued in the seventeenth century; they are still found in the eighteenth century. The decorative effect of these pyramids of fruit is obvious. They usually consisted of several layers of fruit or similar edible items that are decorative in themselves on cups or bowls placed one above the other. These constructions were very short-lived, because the food was soon devoured.

In Desportes's painting the pyramid consists of two beautiful dishes with gadrooned rims and, at the top, a plate separating the peaches from the grapes, apricots and figs. This impressive centrepiece is very effectively set off by a magnificent dish with a gadrooned outer edge and egg-shaped decorations around the inner rim, situated directly behind the piece itself, and two oblong dishes with ornate cut surfaces around their borders. In front of these oblong dishes and flanking the centrepiece are two great ewers decorated with mythological figures and scenes together with their basins. These two ewers are very reminiscent of the famous silver furnishings made in the workshops of the Gobelins and the Louvre, which for the most part disappeared before the end of Louis XIV's reign. Some fruit placed with apparent carelessness on a serviette and a plate of ham emphasize the illusion of still life in the picture and form a pleasant break in the symmetry. On the upper level several vases made of semi-precious stones are set among the decorative sculpture on the marble dresser. There are also two China bowls and, in the centre, a soup-tureen with handles in the form of chimeras. This, like the two ewers on the lower level of the sideboard, is a masterpiece of Louis XIV silverware. As in the case of the centrepiece on the lower level, two oblong dishes with hollow-ribbed edges form a very effective background. The whole display is enlivened by garlands of flowers descending like a waterfall from the top of the buffet, encircling the silver objects and creating a link between the silver and the garden.

When the richly decorated tables so fashionable in the eighteenth century gradually lost favour, the silver sideboard also ceased to be so important. It finally disappeared at the beginning of the nineteenth century. The only examples that survived were the simple dressers that were required for serving meals.

Part II

Table Silverware in Illustrations of Table Settings from the Sixteenth to the Nineteenth Century

It is not so easy as it might at first seem to reproduce by means of selected illustrations the art of setting a table with silver objects. This is partly because artists have never been particularly fond of representing the most common events in everyday life and, at least until the beginning of the eighteenth century, the table rarely presented a scene worthy of an artist's special interest. Even in the most exalted spheres of society, the non-utilitarian art of the table has been concerned only with presenting various dishes in a monumental and often artistic way. It is clearly a very short-lived art form. The sideboard or dresser has in fact been the only really effective means of setting out silverware, the amount and quality of which has inevitably varied according to the house.

We have to wait until the early eighteenth century before the sideboard ceased to be so widely used and gradually came to be replaced by the table as a means for displaying silver. It was then that objects were first taken down from the high shelves and tiers of silver sideboards and placed on tables, which at the same time became more lavishly provided. The table laid and served in this way thus acquired a new dimension. It became decorative. Countless new silver utensils were invented to delight the guests, to make serving effortless and to add luxury to the table. This new fashion was also the reason for the sudden appearance of an impressive number of pictures illustrating tables prepared for meals. There was a clear recognition that laid and served tables were interesting enough to be preserved for posterity.

From these very revealing pictures I have chosen a number of views of tables originating in different countries and social environments and at different periods between the sixteenth and nineteenth centuries. Most of them, for the reasons given above, are from the eighteenth century onwards. With the help of these illustrations, the reader may be able to set silver objects, which are nowadays all too frequently isolated in the artificial luxury of show-cases and therefore often wrongly interpreted, in their original context.

The Faesch Family of Basle at Table, 1559

In the sixteenth century the table set for a royal or princely family differed very little from that of a prosperous middle-class merchant. The only real difference would have been in the ceremonial and the formalities surrounding the service of the meal. One of the earliest pieces of pictorial evidence of a commoner's table, rather than a nobleman's, can be seen in the Fine Arts Museum in Basle, Switzerland. The artist is Hans Hug Kluber and his painting is a little naive, but it is very precise and a great deal can be learned from it.

It shows the family of Hans Rudolf Faesch, who was a rich merchant, a master of a guild and an important person in Basle at the time. The habits and customs at table in a citizen's household during the second half of the sixteenth century that can be seen in this detailed picture were confirmed a few years later by Michel de Montaigne in his *Carnet de Voyage*, written after a long tour of the most famous spas in Europe. Montaigne was particularly struck by the opulence and luxury with which the wealthy merchants of the great Protestant city on the Rhine surrounded themselves, especially at meal times.

Protestantism urged restraint in dress and personal appearance, but was not opposed to a display of luxury inside the home. Silver, which had been both rare and costly throughout the Middle Ages, had become much more easily obtainable as a result of the huge imports of the metal from America since the beginning of the sixteenth century. The price of silver fell correspondingly. This fall coincided with the ban imposed by the Reformers on all excessive luxury in the worship of God. Silversmiths lost their best customer, the pre-Reformation Church, and were obliged to look for new outlets for their wares. They found them among private individuals,

10   The family of Hans Rudolf Faesch at table in 1559. Detail of painting by Hans ▷
Hug Kluber (1535-78). Kunstmuseum, Basle. 4649.

especially those who had recently acquired wealth, had achieved middle-class status, and were anxious to lead a more refined way of life.

In the panelled hall with its great glazed windows and its splendidly tiled floor, a table is set for the family meal, which is taking place before our eyes. There is no dresser with a display of silverware to be seen in this room, but on the table itself is a remarkable collection of silver articles. They must have cost as much as any that graced the tables of the most wealthy families of the period. The table is covered with a fine linen cloth on which these objects are arranged in an obvious order. The people are either sitting or standing, according to their age. In front of each of them is a trencher. This was a circular wooden cutting-board or platter, often decorated on one side with a painting. Such trenchers were in common use until the seventeenth century, but very few have survived. The trencher is the prototype of the individual plate, which, although it was often in use by this time in Italy, had still not been adopted north of the Alps. Each person at table would put a slice of bread cut with his knife on to his trencher and prepare and cut up his meat. Having removed the smaller bones with the same knife, he would then dip the pieces in the salt and take it to his mouth, using either the tip of the blade or simply his fingers. Forks were hardly known at the time: not until some fifty years later did they make a first timid appearance in this part of Europe. The knives with pointed blades were not at this time in matching sets. They were still strictly personal and individual. Each person taking part in the meal would place his own knife where he was sitting at the beginning of the meal. At this period men usually carried daggers with richly decorated hilts and scabbards. The scabbards frequently also contained one or two little table knives. Women often had, in addition to bags and purses hanging from their girdles, elegant quiver-shaped cases containing implements that could be used at table. These objects were frequently baptismal gifts which the child kept until it reached adulthood. In the sixteenth century at least they seem to have been a Swiss or German speciality.

Meals eaten at this period were very monotonous, so that great importance was attached to salt and various spices. They were regarded as indispensable, but were very expensive. They were therefore carefully preserved, used sparingly and presented ceremonially. These three requirements were satisfied when the condiments were kept in a container in the form of a powder-flask. We may assume that the two silver flasks that can be seen on the table contained pepper, nutmeg or cloves, the three spices most in demand in this part of Europe. The little pot in the foreground, with its long silver spout and gilt decoration, has a very Gothic aspect. It must have held mustard, which at the time was served in liquid form, as a kind of sauce.

The drinks consumed were clearly all contained in goblets or hanaps of precious metal. The senior member of the family can be seen holding a silver-gilt cup with a stem. It is richly chased and engraved; on the rim is an indication that it was one of a pair of twin hanaps of the type known in German-speaking countries as 'Willkomm'. The four other rather squat cups with bases clearly form part of a set; it might have consisted of as many as a dozen pieces which could be fitted one inside the other to form an elegant column with a finely wrought cover on top. Only a few examples of this kind of cup have survived intact, however, since the sets were divided up again and again in the course of time. Finally, there is a place left empty in the foreground of the picture. This is in accordance with a practice common in Protestant homes. A place at table was set aside for the Saviour, who was expected to arrive at any moment to share the family's meal.

This taste for silverware was to continue until the eighteenth century in wealthy middle-class circles in German-speaking countries. Tea, coffee and similar drinks were fairly slow to reach these countries from the colonies, but they eventually came to be consumed at various times throughout the day and the habit of drinking a great deal at mealtimes was consequently abandoned. This led to wine and beer being drunk from smaller glasses in the Latin manner.

A Meal of the Bodmer Family of Zurich, 1643

The Swiss cantons had for a long time been separated from the Empire and their inhabitants' way of life and practices at table therefore continued to be strongly Germanic until well into the seventeenth century. There were no kings or princes whose constantly evolving table manners the middle-class citizens of these cantons could imitate, and no changing courtly fashions that they could copy. As a result the art of the table evolved very slowly indeed and remained wedded to family and local traditions. The only important stimuli to development were the increasing wealth of the middle class in the sixteenth and seventeenth centuries and the growing importance of the rich merchant guilds, which were the most powerful institutions in the towns of Switzerland. This led to greater ostentation and refinement at table. One significant practice, already referred to in the last chapter, was that new members were only admitted to these guilds on condition that they presented a gift of a piece of silverware—usually a more or less finely wrought cup—that was as expensive as they could afford. This practice allowed the guilds to accumulate astonishing treasures of silver, which remained untouched until the fall of the Ancien Régime at the end of the eighteenth century and have suffered no serious losses since that time.

These silver objects were set out on tables and dressers whenever guild banquets were held—and this happened quite frequently. In this way the well-to-do citizens of the great Swiss towns who were invited as guests acquired a taste for luxurious silver and began to build up their own family collections, following the example of the guilds. There are, it seems, far more archives and other written documents providing us with lists of these collections than pictures or illustrations. However, one delightful picture, dated 1643, shows the Bodmer family of Zurich at table. It gives a rather naive, but undoubtedly truthful insight into their customs. The contemporary engraving by Conrad Meyer of Zurich, made in 1645 and entitled *Tischzucht* or 'Table Manners', also provides valuable evidence.

11   The Bodmer family of Zurich at table, 1643. Painting by an anonymous artist. Private collection.

In the first of these pictures we see the whole Bodmer family—father, mother and twelve children—gathered around a great rectangular table covered with a white linen cloth decorated with strips of embroidery and a lace edging. The girls are seated on their mother's side of the table and the sons are seated on their father's side, in order of age and according to the practice in votive pictures at the end of the Middle Ages and during the Renaissance. In front of each member of the family is a thick circular wooden platter or trencher. This, as we have already seen, was the precursor of the plate. The food was cut up on these trenchers with the help of the little knives with pointed blades that can be seen on the right of each trencher, the point of the blade being generally employed to convey the pieces of meat to the mouth. The knife was also widely used in another not very attractive way—as a tooth-pick. Cardinal Richelieu so disliked this practice that he not only strenuously forbade it but also obliged everyone to use knives with rounded tips.

Forks were not common in France at this time, but they seem to have been fashionable in the Swiss cantons, which were closer to Venice and Italy, where they were in current use. Only the sons of the Bodmer family have little forks with two short prongs alongside their knives. The daugthers do not seem to have been allowed forks. The parents are using more modern ones with two long prongs and twisted handles, the typical seventeenth-century Swiss fork.

The spoons have a deep circular bowl and a short curved handle. Both in their shape and in the use to which they were put, they are fully in accordance with most spoons in this part of Europe from the early sixteenth century onwards. In the picture they are laid out in two sets, one on each side of the main dish. The children would each take up one of these spoons as soon as the time came to eat. This arrangement of spoons was also traditional. Only the parents are complying with a fashion that was just beginning in Switzerland, that of having one's own spoon together with a knife and fork. The parents' spoons can be seen lying with the rest of their cutlery on a serviette that is folded quite artistically to the right of their trenchers. Like their forks, their spoons also have long, twisted handles, which enabled one to avoid soiling the great ruff around one's neck. Towards the middle of the seventeenth century Swiss women gradually ceased to carry their knives, forks and spoons in a little case and their menfolk gave up the dagger or *Schweizerdolch* in favour of little cases containing their personal cutlery. The great novelty here was the individual spoon.

In Switzerland meals were always accompanied by various drinks—water for children and wine or beer for adults. These drinks were not served as they were in the Latin countries—from a

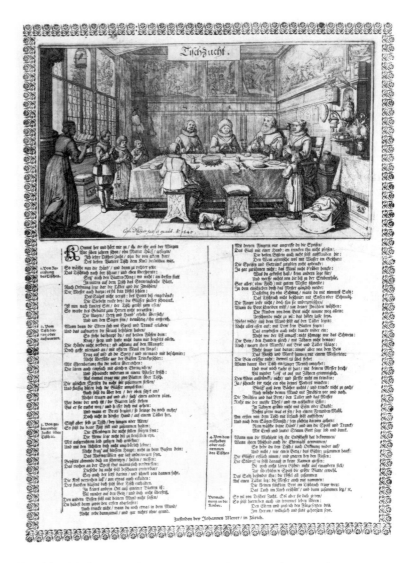

12   A Zurich family at table, 1645. Detail of engraving by Conrad Meyer. Private collection.

buffet or sideboard—but at the table itself. That is why the little hanap with a lid and a gadrooned base is set in front of the father's place. The finial in the shape of a little figure enabled the lid to be raised. This squat type of hanap was far from modern in the mid-seventeenth century—it may even go back to the first half of the preceding century. The use of outdated pieces of silverware points to a certain affectation and also to the antiquity of the family's fortune! Out-of-date objects were greatly revered and carefully preserved in German-speaking countries and in England. In Latin countries, on the other hand, fashion was followed assiduously and new pieces of silverware in strict accordance with current taste were constantly being produced.

This respect for articles that had long since ceased to be fashionable is clearly illustrated in the little tankard in front of the mother. Unlike those in Germany or other northern European countries, which could reach enormous proportions, such receptacles always remained very small in Switzerland. They were, moreover, mainly used by women. Often they were given as wedding presents, decorated with the coats of arms of the two families that were joined together or with biblical themes.

The widespread practice of drinking lukewarm wine and beer led to the use of metal in preference to glass drinking vessels and to the provision of lids on tankards or metal cups. Children only drank cold water and therefore did not require cups with lids. The Bodmer children have little goblets with bases of a type common in Switzerland and Germany from the end of the sixteenth century until the eighteenth. These sets of identical goblets generally had twelve pieces which could be placed one inside the other to form a cylinder, as we saw in the case of the Faesch family's vessels. In the picture each goblet is mounted on a little pedestal decorated with a moulding. The cylindrical cup and its base form a single unit. The vessel is slightly wider at the top. The rim was often engraved and might bear a flange or lip with a discreet moulding.

There is quite a precise arrangement in the centre of the table, consisting of a bowl, spoons, two loaves of bread and two silver salts of a design common in seventeenth-century Europe. They are shaped like a goldsmith's cupel mounted on a moulded circular base, and have a fluted shaft.

Several other pieces of silverware can be seen on the three-tiered dresser in this Zurich interior: two other cups, a vase of flowers, and a strange little ewer with an articulated handle hanging from a pot-hook. The typical Swiss feeding-bottle or *Sugerli* must have been used in miniature form as a mustard-pot. In a larger size the same object regularly appeared alongside the water-fountain or cistern until the beginning of the nineteenth century. It contained scented water for rinsing out one's mouth.

The Great Cover for the Marriage of Maria Teresa of Austria and Francis of Lorraine, 12 February 1736

Although it was known as the 'Great Cover', this manner of setting the table for royal occasions in Europe from the seventeenth to the nineteenth century was in fact a surprisingly simple arrangement. It was, of course, accompanied by an elaborate and ostentatious ceremonial and it was perhaps this which never failed to impress those members of the court who were permitted to take part in it or watch it. Courtiers eagerly sought the honour of an invitation to this spectacle, which was fundamentally a Baroque stage production in which the royal person was presented. What is perhaps strange is that no illustration of this important event in the life of the court, which reached its climax in the reign of Louis XIV, has come down to us. The only pictures of royal meals that still exist are those reproduced in the various sets of engravings of royal anointings and coronations. These unfortunately provide no details of the way the table was set or the silver with which it might have been decorated. This silence is probably deliberate—it was no doubt seen as wrong to draw attention to objects on the table and away from the monarch, who had to be the sole focal point.

The etiquette surrounding the Great Cover was evolved in the Middle Ages and very few changes were made in it throughout the whole period of the monarchy, only a few refinements being added. One essential article was always found on the table: the nef or cadenas (the locked container holding the king's knife, fork and spoon and his bread, serviette and spices).

Among the few illustrations of these royal meals is the representation of the Great Cover prepared at the Hofburg in Vienna for the marriage of Maria Teresa of Austria. This surprisingly little-known picture not only gives us a good idea of the ceremonial of a royal meal, but also offers a fine opportunity to examine the silverware that adorned the table on that occasion.

The Emperor Charles VI and his wife, who are presiding at the great square table, are seated under a baldachin. On one side of them is the bridal couple and on the other are the bride's aunt and sister. The table is still set according to the seventeenth-century fashion and has no purely decorative silver, but only those pieces used in the service of the meal. In the middle is a large circular pie studded with branches of orange blossom and placed on a folded serviette lying on a silver dish. On each side of this dish is what appears to be a little tureen with handles and a lid. These tureens are also placed on salvers protected by serviettes. I have not been able to ascertain for sure whether these two pieces were in fact cadenas of a special shape replacing the imperial silver nefs often featured on royal tables. In the foreground are two ladies in full court dress who are arranging dishes and utensils, the most interesting of which is a large soup-spoon with violin-scroll handle.

The guests are eating a dish that appears to be oysters, to judge from the little bowls like goldsmiths' cupels that are held so

28

delicately by the Empress or from the lemon which the duke is squeezing. The individual place settings consisted traditionally of gold utensils for monarchs and silver-gilt for the others present; the utensils consist here of a plate, spoon and knife. There is no fork on the imperial table. It is quite likely that the fork, which was for a long time overlooked and even forbidden by court etiquette, was deliberately excluded from this solemn occasion.

It does not take many years for table settings as simple as this one in the Viennese Hofburg to be forgotten. Enormous progress was to be made in luxury in the next decades and soon tables like that of the Emperor Charles VI in 1736 would be found only in middle-class homes.

The Cake of Kings and the Wedding Feast of People of Rank: Two Middle-Class Tables of the Mid-Eighteenth Century

What we have learned from the three examples given so far is that, in the sixteenth and seventeenth and even in first part of the eighteenth centuries, royal tables did not differ fundamentally from those of middle-class citizens. As the eighteenth century proceeded, however, this changed. Because of a certain desire to be faithful to tradition, the royal cover continued to be quite modest on most occasions. The Baroque era, however, was also an age of sumptuous and ostentatious banquets in which a family's whole silver collection would be prominently displayed. Much of the magnificent silverware of this period has disappeared, but many upper middle-class families still possess, and often use, a number of fine table objects that go back to the eighteenth century. In this section we shall consider two engravings which show dining-rooms that were quite typical of the mid-eighteenth century, one in Paris and the other in the Netherlands.

The first in an engraving entitled *Le Gateau des Roys*, copied from a picture by Philippe Canot (*c.* 1750). It shows a simple Parisian family. In the foreground a meal is taking place in a room furnished in a plain, unaffected way. A female servant is bringing in a steaming stew in an earthenware bowl and is about to place it on a circular wickerwork stand bearing a silver coaster, of a magnificent kind well known at the time in English-speaking countries. Each

14 *Le Gateau des Roys*. Print by J.P. Lebas, based on a picture by Philippe Canot, *c.* 1750. Cabinet des Estampes, Bibliothèque Nationale, Paris.

place has a china or porcelain plate and there are knives, forks and spoons scattered at random beside the plates. The parents each have a stemmed glass in front of their plates, since they clearly have no man-servant to bring the drinks, as was the custom at this time. Fifty years later glasses would generally form part of the table setting. The child has his own beaker, which would normally have been a baptismal gift. Here it can be seen just in front of his place. A large serving spoon is lying in the middle of the table.

The doors of the large cupboard or dresser in the background are open, allowing us to see the rest of the table-ware. If it is of silver, it is clearly of a kind that was both rare and unpretentious. It is not certain, however, whether it is of silver, pewter or even porcelain, since objects in all three materials at that period had the same shape and design. The contents of the cupboard include several dishes of

various sizes, a number of chamber candlesticks and one tall candlestick or *flambeau*, another serving spoon and a set of cruets. There is nothing in this collection that would have been found in a more wealthy home.

The second of these two pictures is by the Swiss engraver Daniel Herrliberger (1697-1777) and shows us a much more opulent interior in the Netherlands at about the same time. The scene is that of a family banquet—as is clear from the title: 'A Wedding Feast of People of Rank'.

15 *A Wedding Feast of People of Rank*, showing a family meal *c.* 1740. Engraving by Daniel Herrliberger (1697-1777).

Eleven places are set around the great round table. In the middle are three large dishes of food ready to be eaten by those present, each of whom has a plate, a knife with a very large blade, and a meat-fork. It is clearly the type of fork that was used both to cut up meat and to convey it to the mouth, for it has two long steel prongs.

The spoon is placed horizontally above the plate, but it is not possible to identify the type of handle with any certainty in this engraving. The glasses are of a type that was extremely popular in the Low Countries from the seventeenth century onwards. They were undoubtedly brought by a man-servant on a silver salver, but they were not emptied at once and here can be seen standing with nothing between them and the table-cloth. The only other piece of silverware on the table is a little mustard-cruet. At the end of the room on the right a servant is carving a young pig, helped by a maid who is holding out the plates that she will serve. The wall on the other side of the door at the back of the room is taken up by a large cupboard with glass-panelled doors, behind which can be seen many pieces of table-ware. Much of it could only have been made of silver, although its quality is not a sure guide that this was so.

Because there is such a striking similarity between what can be seen in these two engravings, especially the first, and customs that are still common today, we shall henceforth not consider table arrangements of a more modest kind. These have little to contribute to our knowledge of the history of silverware, which has always been mainly confined to more wealthy homes.

The Reception of the Elector of Cologne in Venice, 1755

In Italy, despite the fact that the silversmith's craft was almost everywhere held in greater esteem than any other form of decorative art, there was a certain reticence, not only in the seventeenth century but even in the eighteenth, towards displays of table silverware that were common at the time in northern Europe. Less importance was attached to the real value of materials in the Italian cities during the eighteenth century than at any other time in their history. What mattered to their citizens then was the illusion or the dreamlike quality of the decorative effect that the artist was able to draw out of his material by exercising his skill. It was at this period of Italian art that the taste for illusion reached its zenith.

Such a view was clearly not favourable to any form of art that involved the amassing of treasure in the form of solid silver. The silversmith's art was rejected and there was a clear preference for novel forms of decoration of a more ephemeral kind. This attitude in Italy was in striking contrast to that prevalent in England and Germany. The Italians preferred light but dazzlingly rich silver objects to solid but basically simple ones. In every case the desire for ostentation determined the nature of the work and that is why the fashion for silver sideboards persisted for so long in Italy.

In Italy as in Spain, finely wrought solid silverware was above all made for the Church. Despite this, Italian pre-eminence in the sphere of art led to a gradual refinement in table manners all over Europe. It was for the Italian courts of the Middle Ages and the Renaissance that table-ware of satisfactory aesthetic quality was first produced. More usually this was of porcelain or glass rather than gold or silver. For a long time Venice was the link between East and West and it was here that sophisticated table manners developed long before they did in other Italian cities. The fork, for example, gradually but irresistibly spread from Venice to the rest of the continent.

Italian painters have never been as concerned as those in northern Europe to reproduce the details that can provide us with information on our subject. It would be good to know more about how Italians of different social status behaved at table and what silver they used. Unfortunately, it is clear from contemporary works that they were more interested in the artistic presentation of dishes in the form of real, but of course very ephemeral, works of sculpture composed of edible items. If beautiful silver treasures existed, they were hardly ever removed from the shelves of the sideboards that were so highly esteemed in Italy.

The delightful painting by an artist employed by the Longhi family of Venice is probably simple and ingenuous enough to give us a very exact insight into the magnificence of one Venetian banquet organized for notable citizens in the mid-eighteenth century. This feast took place in the Nanni Palace on 9 September 1755 in honour of the Elector of Cologne, the well-known Clement Augustus, who had built the splendid residence at Brühl. The Elector was very fickle and was clearly seeking amusement in Venice. One form of entertainment was this extremely sumptuous banquet.

The long table with places for more than a hundred guests on both sides is set out in the form of a horseshoe in a great hall well illuminated by a series of large bay-windows and, as night falls, by the light of great chandeliers. It is typical of Italy at this period that, despite the high rank of the principal guest, no serious attempt is made to achieve elegance. The host has not even taken the trouble to match all the pieces of the dinner-service—some of the plates are of silver, while others are silver-gilt! The great table is almost

16   A banquet given for the Elector of Cologne at the Palazzo Nanni in Venice, ▷ 1755. Painting by an artist of the School of Longhi. Ca' Rezzonico, Venice.

17   A meal at the Prince of Conti's townhouse, the Temple, Paris, 1766. Painting ▷▷ by M.-B. Ollivier (d. 1784). Château de Versailles.

empty and there is no fine silverware, only dishes containing food; they are not even covered and are placed here and there by men-servants waiting at table. Perhaps the painter simply failed to record the truth here, but not all the guests have utensils at their places to enable them to eat decently! Knives, forks and spoons are missing from many places. Wine-glasses and carafes are set out on silver coasters which the waiters have placed on the table or are offering to the guests. They have taken them from a dresser that has been specially prepared in the recess on the right of the picture. Servants are busy in this alcove pouring wine into decanters and diluting it with water contained in great ewers. There are bread-baskets placed at regular intervals on the table, but there is no sign of any salt-cellars.

At the end of the table, close to the Elector, is a buffet with a shelf on which silver-gilt dishes and several fine ewers are displayed. At this buffet the servants are looking after the dishes that have been brought from the pantry or are being returned there. Many spectators are pressing forward on the raised platform at this end of the hall and looking down. Their view of the scene must have been impressive, but the setting of the table is certainly inferior.

Italian silverware was obviously no longer at the height of its glory at this time. Several decades later artists like Valadier were sufficiently stimulated by examples from imperial France to try to have great silver centrepieces accepted in Italian circles. Napoleon liked to have these centrepieces in the many Italian palaces that he had arranged for himself, although almost all of them remained at the planning stage. Megalomania was not at all in keeping with a country that had been bled white and shaken to its foundations by revolution. In such a condition great works of art in silver could not be produced.

A Choice Supper at the Prince of Conti's in the Paris Temple, 1766

In France in the last decade of the seventeenth century great changes were made in the way in which the table was set. Louis XIV always clung to tradition in such matters and even perfected court table etiquette with the intention of preserving the established order unchanged. He let himself be shackled in this way in order to protect his royal person from the nobles' influence and to deify his own function as much as possible in his subjects' eyes. With the passage of time, however, this isolation became oppressive and to escape from it the king created little islands of intimacy in his residences of Trianon and Marly. He lived there like a great lord, but the luxury that surrounded him, although very ostentatious, was less oppressive than at Versailles and novelties were not excluded.

It was in these two residences and in the smaller courts of members of the royal family at St. Cloud, Meudon, Sceaux and Chantilly, or in their Paris homes, that table settings became an extremely refined art. At the turn of the seventeenth and eighteenth centuries silverware was taken down from the shelves of the sideboards to which it had been relegated and appeared more and more frequently on the table itself. Many new objects were created. During the Regency a new class, a rich bourgeoisie, emerged. Fortunes were gained and these people wanted to show off their new wealth. This taste for display was often expressed in the richly adorned tables of the new aristocrats. There are many eighteenth-century descriptions of astonishing meals, but very few illustrations offer details of the choice dinners and light suppers given by Louis XV, Madame de Pompadour or the financiers and tax farmers of the ancien régime.

Nevertheless Ollivier's attractive picture contains a great deal of information about what silver objects were used and how they were distributed on fashionable tables in the eighteenth century. The meal is taking place in a room with painted panelling in the Temple, one of the most luxurious townhouses in Paris at the time. The great rectangular table in the foreground is occupied by a number of guests and musicians. The great innovation here is that no servant or waiter is to be seen. The painter has chosen to depict the scene during the dessert—the main dishes have already been served and consumed. The only decorative element on the table is the great centrepiece. It consists of a great salver of mirrors, in the midst of which is a silver composition decorated with figurines. Are these of the same kind as those that can now be seen in the Museum of Fine Arts in Lisbon? Tall candles, set in sockets which seem to be drip-receivers, are arranged round the edge of the centrepiece after the fashion of the eminent specialist Jacques Helft. Were they perhaps not simply fixed to short candelabra arms attached to the outer rim?

The guests are eating fruit on plates made of china without using knives or forks, which had undoubtedly been taken away with the previous course. The stemmed glasses are placed upside down in little individual wine-glass coolers. The bottles, on the other hand, are kept in ice in larger wine-coolers placed on little tables. These occasional tables take the place of servants. They are set close to the dining-table between the guests and contain everything that the latter might need at the end of the meal.

The table at the back of the alcove on the left is arranged according to an identical plan. The greatest difference is in the way in which it is lighted—two pairs of tall candlesticks, baluster-shaped. Instead of a centrepiece four silver dishes full of fruit of various kinds and cakes have been placed in the middle of the table. There is also a supplementary table beside this dining-table in the alcove and on it are two large wine-coolers filled with bottles of wine.

It is not easy for us nowadays to imagine the semi-darkness in which even the most comfortably placed members of society lived in the eighteenth century once night had fallen. Electricity has accustomed us to an almost excessive brightness in our homes, halls and dining-rooms and this has perhaps made us forget the practical function served by table silverware in earlier centuries as a reflector of light.

A Plan for a Table Arrangement, *c.* 1770

The eighteenth-century art of setting a table with many places can be traced back not only to the taste and ability of the host or his steward, but also very frequently to the skill of an expert. Perhaps a

18   Plan of a table arrangement, France, *c.* 1770. Musée des Arts Décoratifs, Paris. A 8957.

painter or architect, depending on the degree of importance of the house, he was required to draw up a detailed table plan and to design an arrangement of magnificent pieces to decorate the table for the occasion. These plans were never made to be preserved and handed down to posterity. Their purpose was to increase the enjoyment of a particular banquet.

The anonymous plan for fifty places preserved in the collection of the Musée des Arts Décoratifs in Paris is one of the few surviving examples. I believe that it illustrates more clearly than any other such picture the detailed care devoted to table arrangements at this time.

The basic characteristic of the French type of service was that all the dishes were placed on the table before the diners arrived. The central part of the great oblong table is arranged in the form of a flower-bed such as could be found in the very regular French gardens of the time, surrounding three massive plinths or projections which were no doubt composed in the style of architectural monuments. The first enclosure is formed of different parts of a table-runner decorated according to two different plans, between which the organizer of the banquet could choose.

The flower-beds, vases of flowers and allegorical attributes were undoubtedly made on a foundation of mirrors covered with coloured sand. These extraordinary sand decorations were very popular about 1770. At regular intervals around this first section

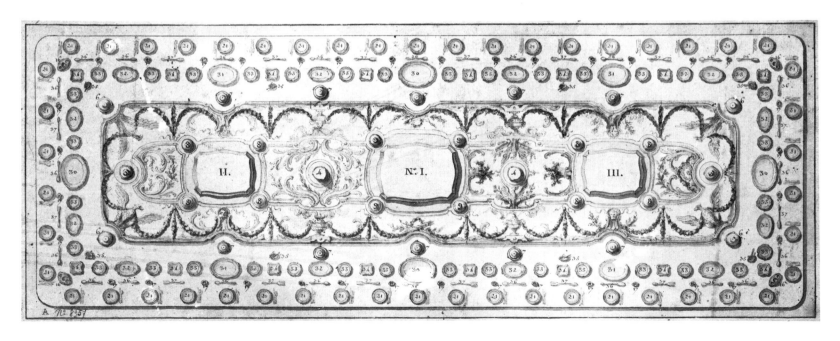

pieces of silverware were undoubtedly placed. The circles enclosing numbers on the plan may indicate candlesticks, candelabra, tureens, dish-covers or figurines on stands.

The second enclosure is arranged in very similar way, with attributes in the same taste and with garlands of flowers and leaves. The circles may stand for tureens or dish-covers. Unfortunately, the key has not been preserved and so we can only guess what silver or other objects were placed in the centre of the table.

The other objects arranged around the outer edge can, however, be identified with some certainty. The numbers referring to the dishes do not follow each other regularly. It can therefore be assumed that this particular plan was part of a set of plans for a meal consisting of several courses and that the missing numbers on this plan may stand for dishes in earlier courses. Here we have a clear arrangement of four different types of dish set out around the table. There are large oblong dishes, smaller dishes in the same shape, bowls and vegetable dishes. Set out at regular intervals are sauce-boats with spoons, a great number of serving spoons and something that must have been remarkably rare at the time, serving forks following each other in a chain, alternating with the serving spoons, between the dishes and the plates. A set of cruets is placed at each corner of the table. The setting for each diner accords with Spanish convention: that is to say, a matching set of a spoon, fork and knife is placed to the right of each plate. There are also individual salt-cellars in front of each place. Glasses are not to be seen on the table, for the guests would ask their servants for drinks as they required them. They would not place the glasses on the table but would dilute their wine with water from a decanter.

This particularly French service resulted in a magnificent table setting, but it led to serious difficulties. It was obviously not easy to change all the dishes set out on the table with each new course and the diners would be disturbed by the interminable coming and going of the servants. It is therefore not difficult to appreciate that the so-called Russian form of service, which was to let those present pass the dishes from one to another in accordance with a strict order of propriety, was adopted with alacrity.

The Banquet at the Marriage of the Archduke Joseph of Austria and Princess Isabella of Parma at the Vienna Hofburg, 1760

There are many detailed descriptions but relatively few really good illustrations of the banquets which every European court was so fond of giving from the Middle Ages onwards. All the rulers of the Baroque age knew that it was on occasions of this kind that they were seen in the most favourable light. Their subjects were also generally allowed to pass in front of the table at which they were seated and on show. A record of these great meals has been preserved for posterity both in popular prints and in engravings and paintings of good quality made in the eighteenth century. In particular, a set of huge compositions by Martin van Meytens (1695-1770) and his pupils gives an excellent impression of various important historical events marking the development of the relationship between the houses of Bourbon and Habsburg. The Empress Maria Teresa was understandably very proud of this relationship and wanted to commemorate it in a series of paintings illustrating, among other things, court banquets. Our picture shows the French form of service in all its splendour and is full of detail.

The artist was obviously not able to reproduce several different courses of the banquet on one canvas. He therefore decided to depict the first course with its brilliant display of the superb table silverware of the Viennese court. It hardly needs to be said that many other courts—those of Versailles, St. Petersburg, Madrid, Dresden or Lisbon, for example—undoubtedly had silver treasures of similar splendour, but we have no comparable illustration of these collections.

The scene is set in the great antechamber of the Hofburg Palace. It is the wedding-day of the Archduke and future Emperor Joseph II. The members of the imperial family are seated on three sides of an arrangement of tables. The Emperor Francis of Lorraine and the Empress Maria Teresa of Austria preside over the table. On each side of the sovereigns are the archdukes and archduchesses who belong to the imperial family.

Banqueting-tables were at this period always formed of boards that were made especially to the measurements required by the hall and the number of guests; they were set on trestles. This case is certainly no exception: the trestle-tables are set out in the form of a rectangle with a gap opposite the imperial baldachin. The staff responsible for serving the dishes pass through the gap into the rectangular enclosure and serve different parts of the table. The diners are seated on the outside only, where they are clearly visible and can be admired by those allowed to watch this gala dinner.

19 Banquet given on the occasion of the marriage of the future Joseph II and ▷ Princess Isabella of Parma at the Vienna Hofburg, 1760. Detail of painting by Martin van Meytens (1695-1770). Schloss Schönbrunn, Vienna.

Nothing is visible of the trestles and boards, which are completely hidden beneath a crimson velvet or damask table-cover and at least two white cloths placed one on top of the other. It was the practice to remove the soiled table-cloth at the end of each course, the last being revealed when the dessert was served.

The two sovereigns are seated under the great canopy, draped with a magnificent fabric. At the Emperor's side is the Archduke Joseph, the bridegroom, and opposite him is his bride. The rest of the family is seated in order of precedence. The table is decorated with a magnificent set of dishes and other silver-gilt objects. In accordance with the etiquette governing the Great Cover, the table-ware is arranged in such a way that the diners are never hidden behind large objects that would prevent them being seen by the spectators.

The banquet must have been held in daylight, because there are no candlesticks to impede the service of a great number of busy servants in red livery and the movement of the members of the staff and high-ranking dignitaries of the court. The latter are dressed in the traditional black livery imposed by Spanish protocol, which was adopted by the Viennese court in the sixteenth century. It consisted of padded trunk-hose and a short black cape. The staff had the task of handing dishes to the diners who asked for them. These were set out according to the order laid down by the French form of service. They did not necessarily correspond to the taste of every guest who found himself seated near a particular dish.

The upper part of the table at which the Emperor and Empress are seated forms the central point of the symmetrical composition. It is not difficult to distinguish, among the silverware, many vessels, tureens, bowls and dishes without lids, which together form a single whole. A great centrepiece surmounted by a basket of fruit is in the middle of the upper table. The tureens are of various kinds, but are all presented on salvers which remain on the table. When one is brought to the table, its lid is held down by means of a folded napkin, following the medieval custom. They are uncovered and presented to the diners, who serve themselves from them, using great serving spoons. These spoons were arranged on the table-cloth between the dishes and the diners' plates before the meal began.

All these places are set with identical plates forming part of the same service, although it is possible that the sovereigns' plates and utensils are of gold, to distinguish them from those of the others present, which in that case would have been of silver-gilt. The plates had a delicately shaped inner rim, and were never placed on

top of one another. Each place also has a three-pronged fork, a knife with a steel blade and a spoon, all three with silver-gilt handles; the whole set of cutlery was not arranged in any strict order. There is a bread roll and an individual covered box containing spices beside each person's place. In this little box there would have been two compartments, one for salt and the other for ground pepper. It is clearly the descendant, very much reduced in size and style, of the earlier cadenas, although here it more resembles a snuff-box. In this context it is worth pointing out that many of the little boxes now often described as snuff-boxes are in fact really individual spice-boxes. As always on such an important table, there are no glasses.

This is an exceptionally brilliant and ostentatious set of table silverware, even for the eighteenth century. Only the richest and most fashionable courts in Europe could claim to possess such silver-plate and many would in any case have preferred to use china-ware at this period. Silver of this kind would, moreover, seldom have been ordered in complete sets. It was more usual for articles to be bought individually or in small amounts, often spread out over several years, depending on the family's needs and the availability of the product.

Nowadays, when most such homogeneous sets of silverware have been divided or destroyed, it is difficult to imagine what a brilliant effect they produced. Many modern collectors assess the aesthetic quality of certain pieces of silver quite wrongly, precisely because of their isolation from the large service of which they once formed part. They cannot easily imagine that the brilliant decorative effect of the whole set was often much more important in the eighteenth century than, for example, the quality of the chasing on an object that was only one among many.

A Supper Given by the Imperial Family in the Hall of the Redoute in Vienna, *c.* 1760

The meal that was arranged to take place with such a display of magnificence on this particular evening in the great Hall of the Redoute was, according to the generally accepted tradition, a supper, like the banquet described above, to celebrate the marriage between the Archduke Joseph and Isabella of Parma in 1760. The difficulty, however, is that although the artist, Martin van Meytens, was well known for his skill as a portraitist the persons shown do not correspond to reality. Neither Joseph nor Isabella are seated in the places reserved for the principal guests, who are represented as

20 *The Great Cover of King Charles III of Spain.* Painting by Luis Paret y Alcazar ◁ (1746-99), *c.* 1760. Prado Museum, Madrid.

much older persons. May not this supper have been a reception held a few years before by the Emperor and Empress for notable guests in the presence of archdukes and duchesses? In the context of our study, the identity of the persons present is of no great importance, since we are concerned merely with the decorative arrangement of the table.

Maria Teresa is reputed to have been extremely fond of all kinds of festivities. This would explain why Martin van Meytens was commissioned to make a permanent record of events at court during the royal couple's reign in vast works of representational art. As was already pointed out, his work is unique in providing us with pictorial evidence. This painting depicts the last part of a gala banquet and to some extent complements the preceding one, which showed the first course, if not of the same meal then of a similar one.

The nocturnal feast is served on covered trestle-tables laid out in the form of a horseshoe in the great Redoutensaal of the Hofburg, which could be adapted according to the requirements of various royal occasions. The Emperor and Maria Teresa are presiding in the centre under a canopy of rich fabric, attended by leading gentlemen of the court. Members of the imperial family are seated along the outer side of each table. On the sovereign's right hand are two unidentified guests of honour. Their importance is emphasized by the respectful distance preserved between them and the archduchesses. As in the previous example, the arrangement of the tables in the form of an open rectangle has the great advantage of allowing the staff, who are dressed in Spanish livery, to enter the central area and serve the guests rapidly.

The meal is clearly approaching its end, since the dishes used in the principal courses have been cleared away and replaced by the centrepiece for the dessert and fruit has been placed within the diners' reach. Each change of service involved a great deal of bustle, but the final one, with its presentation of the centrepiece and the sweet dishes, was always the most laborious. Feasts were planned as if they were dramatic spectacles divided into several acts.

For the last course a runner was laid out along the entire inner length of the table, in an arrangement similar to that of 1770. In our picture the runner consists of a series of mirrors joined together and enclosed within a frame, with little feet in the form of volutes. The main purpose of these mirrors was of course to reflect the candle-light. A household officer, who must have been a specialist in this type of work, has outlined patterns in sand on this foundation. Multicoloured grains of sand were frequently used in these delightful decorations, and tiny coloured sweets were sometimes scattered on the glass as well. These *nonpareilles*, as they

21 Feast at the court of Francis of Lorraine and Maria Teresa of Austria, held in ▷ the Hall of the Redoute, Vienna, *c.* 1760. Detail of painting by Martin van Meytens. Schloss Schönbrunn, Vienna.

were called, are often mentioned in descriptions. This particular table decoration is clearly reminiscent of a flower-bed, laid out like a tapestry in the manner of the French gardens of the period, with here and there little ceramic human figures and tiny comfit-dishes.

Set out at regular intervals along both sides of the runner are thirty-four silver-gilt candlesticks. These not only enhance the brilliant effect of the table but also throw light on the diners. The candles and candlesticks are characteristic of the period: the former are very tall and slender and the latter have no drip-trays.

Between the two rulers is an attractive pyramid of fruit. Plates containing fruit and various delicacies, cups, comfit-dishes and little baskets of confectionery alternate in front of the guests. All the places are identical, thus making the decor a single whole. In accordance with Spanish custom, a silver-gilt fork, knife and spoon, to be used exclusively for the sweet course, are placed on the right-hand side of each plate, which has a delicately wrought inner rim. No drinks are served during this course and so no glasses disturb its arrangement. There is no sign of the practice which became so widespread in the second half of the nineteenth century: that of arranging flowers or floral decorations on the table. Not only flowers, but also large pieces of silverware are absent here.

A Feast Held to Celebrate the Election of the King of the Romans at Frankfurt, 1764

The election of the young Archduke Joseph as King of the Romans in 1764 was marked by a prodigious display of opulence. This can be explained by the fact that his mother, Empress Maria Teresa of Austria, was concerned to ensure by this election that the imperial crown would in the future be handed down to her descendants, despite the fierce opposition by many electors of the Holy Roman Empire. At the same time she wanted to celebrate, in the most brilliant way possible, the end of hostilities between the different electors, who had been fighting each other for so long during the murderous Seven Years' War.

If we are to believe contemporary writers, these aims were to a great extent achieved as a result of the splendid ceremonies that

took place at Frankfurt. Among the many authors who were greatly impressed by the events was the illustrious poet Goethe, who gave a very exact account in his *Wilhelm Meister*. That great cosmopolitan gentleman, the Duke of Croÿ, also left a record of the election in his *Mémoires*, where he draws an interesting comparison between the Frankfurt ceremony and that of anointing the kings of France at Rheims. A very alert observer, he recognized the great solemnity of the anointing ceremony in France, but was none the less quite ready to admit that it was surpassed by the coronation meal at Frankfurt.

This duke's conviction is, in my view, borne out by the astonishing scene depicted in Martin van Meytens's fine painting, one of the most beautiful in the set he composed for the great series of events in the reign of Maria Teresa. This scene seems to have been painted directly from life and is full of details concerning the ceremony itself and its spectacular setting in the Hall of the Romans. More than two centuries later, we are able to watch, as it were, a film of the event. It speaks volumes about the part played by silverware in a great feast of this period and offers a detailed and probably complete list of the objects used.

The great Römersaal, as we see it in this picture, is arranged in accordance with traditional banquet etiquette, which called for eight individual tables for the grand electors to be set out along the walls. Each of these little tables stands out against a background of tall sideboards, full of superb silverware and surmounted by a canopy of a richness appropriate to the rank of grand elector. The electors of second rank have a table with ten places reserved for them in the middle of the hall. The table of the Emperor and King of the Romans resembles a high altar in a church. It overlooks the hall from a stepped dais at the back of the hall. The magnificent tapestry hangings draped in the space between the two windows are surmounted by the imperial baldachin. In accordance with custom, a great buffet and a dresser are placed on each side of the Emperor's table. A third dresser, which is used by the officers serving the meal, is situated in front of a screen of drapery in the middle of the room, opposite the table. The whole hall is full of courtiers and servants moving in different directions between the tables. The guests are not allowed to take their places until the sovereigns have been served. The scene depicted by Martin van Meytens has, of course,

great historical interest. He reproduces faithfully the way in which the tables and buffets were arranged and decorated.

The table to which he devotes the closest attention in that reserved for the electors of second rank. This table, shown in the detail illustrated here, is in the foreground of the scene that is unfolding before our eyes. It is covered by a heavy crimson table-cover and a white cloth. The magnificent silver objects that adorn it clearly form part of a single set. (Only the sovereigns, it is worth noting, are served from gold or silver-gilt table-ware.) In the middle of this table is a centrepiece consisting of a raised salver with a convoluted rim mounted on little feet in the form of volutes. This centrepiece is functional as well as highly decorative and it contains most of the articles needed during the meal. There are, for example, two cruets in silver mountings for oil and vinegar and two silver sugar-casters. At the top of a voluted structure rising from the centre of the base, executed in the extended rocaille style favoured at Augsburg, is a deep recess holding oranges or lemons, arranged as a pyramid with a branch of orange blossom in the middle.

The rest of the service radiates from this centrepiece. The arrangement of four little oblong tureens set on oval salvers, which are probably sauce-boats, four larger tureens of the same design, and four great circular soup-tureens on two-handled salvers is perfectly symmetrical. Four large salts on trumpet-shaped mountings are set out regularly between these essential items.

The table etiquette at the Viennese court was, as we have seen, based on the Spanish model. Here at Frankfurt, however, the places are arranged in accordance with German practice at the time. The plates with delicately shaped rims are all covered with serviettes artistically folded into a cabbage shape. On the right of each plate is a single knife with a steel blade. This was used to cut the meat, held by a fork with two long steel prongs that can be seen on the left of the plate. Next to it is another fork with three short silver prongs curving inwards, which had the sole purpose of conveying the morsels of food to the guest's mouth. The spoon placed horizontally above each plate is turned with its bowl facing the setting and its handle to the right. At one corner of the table is the only serving spoon. In accordance with custom, there are no glasses on the table.

This unique picture has an additional value. It shows us a table of the period before its arrangement has been disturbed by the guests. It can therefore answer all the questions one might ask about the way in which the silverware and the individual places were set out in the eighteenth century.

The smaller individual tables prepared for the grand electors were also set according to the same pattern, although they differed

◁ 22 Feast held to celebrate the election of the King of the Romans, the future Emperor Joseph II, in the Römersaal in Frankfurt, 1764. Painting by Martin van Meytens. Schloss Schönbrunn, Vienna.

slightly from each other. Some, for example, had only one salt, whereas others had two; some had tureens with flat lids and others tureens with domed covers. In all cases, the bread placed on each setting was surrounded or covered by a folded serviette.

The imperial table was set with the greatest attention, in accordance with an ancient ritual. Despite this, it was of exactly the same construction as all the other tables in the hall and consisted of a simple board placed on trestles. These, however, were completely hidden under the table-cover and the cloth.

To judge from the artist's representation, this table is decorated with a strange mixture of modern and traditional objects. A great oblong tureen with two handles stands in the middle between the

23 *Left*: a dresser bearing different hanaps and goblets. Servants are inspecting the food and drinks that are to be served to the sovereigns on whose table are a nef and carving implements. *Charlemagne's Feast*, illuminated manuscript, Brussels, mid-15th century. Koninklijke Bibliotheek, Brussels. MS. No. 9066.

24 Detail of plate 22. ▷

25 Detail of plate 22. ▷▷

two sovereigns. In front of this central tureen is a place with a whole armoury of knives for the officer in charge to carve the meat and poultry ceremoniously so that it can be served at the tables. Only the Emperor has a covered bowl with lugs beside his place. This type of bowl, which was used for tasting clear soup and was already appearing less and less frequently on tables at this time, is a showpiece that is in great demand now. The finest examples were made in Paris, Augsburg and Strasbourg. In front of the two places are the boxes for spices or salts, depending on which condiment was to be used. The rest of the service is in the French tradition and consists of magnificent gold or silver-gilt tureens, either covered or uncovered, prominently displayed on the table.

Many servants can be seen in the picture bringing dishes that are arranged on the sideboards or taking them from the table to these dressers. The kitchens were a long way off and the service was slow. The problem of how to keep the dishes warm was solved partly by using tureens and covered dishes made of silver, which cools very slowly, and partly by serving from large silver canteens. Two examples of a type that is very rare today can be seen in front of the windows at the end of the room. At the base of the sideboards are dressers where drinks are prepared. The servants fill the glasses and decanters and place them on coasters for them to be served to the guests. The drinks were chilled by putting them in great wine-coolers. The picture shows several silver flagons and glass decanters resting in a basin of this kind.

The tall sideboards which occupy the entire height of the wall against which they stand are purely decorative. They are not constructed, as they might have been in the past, according to an elaborate protocol defining the exact number of tiers corresponding to the rank of the person to whom they relate. A hierarchy of materials was, however, observed at this time, with the result that the objects adorning the buffets of the Emperor and King of the Romans were almost exclusively silver-gilt, as they were at the 1760 banquet. Going up from the lowest to the highest level in the picture, there are, above the drinks on the lowest level, a shelf containing several dishes and a great ewer, which might, in an emergency, have been used in the service of the meal; above these two tureens, reflected in their salvers, with a great three-branched candelabrum on each side. In the foreground at this level are two spice-boxes with double lids, and in the middle a centrepiece holding oil-and vinegar-cruets and a basket of fruit, which may have been placed on the Emperor's table during a later course. The tier above contains a huge and rather incongruous kettle without its lamp, with a helmet-shaped ewer and its bowl, dishes and candelabra on either side. These form part of the same silver service

as the pieces below and those above, but the choice appears to be quite arbitrary and they are assembled here simply for decoration. The same applies to the third, fourth and fifth levels of the buffet, which contain tureens, vessels, ewers, flagons, candelabra and hanaps of various kinds.

The silverware collection displayed on the Emperor's buffet in Martin van Meytens's painting is supplemented by the pieces on the other buffets lining the walls of the hall. Together they form an illustrated encyclopaedia of eighteenth-century silverware. The objects on the other sideboards are more varied. Indeed, one would hardly expect to see some of them in such a majestic setting, since pieces that are merely ostentatious are placed beside quite ordinary silver articles that might have been in everyday use. Coffee-pots and other receptacles, silver dishes and sundry table-ware are set out here very much as a shopkeeper might display goods for sale.

This picture, of which I have provided only a detail, gives us an excellent insight into the way in which tables and buffets were adorned and diners and servants behaved in the eighteenth century. It shows the context and original function of the pieces of silverware that I have attempted to describe and evaluate individually here.

King Gustavus III of Sweden at Dinner, *c.* 1773

In the eighteenth century Swedish art in general and Swedish silverware in particular were often based on French models. From the beginning of that century rulers followed the ceremonial of Versailles at their own court and sent artists to France to gather detailed information. A study of the pictures preserved in Swedish royal collections may tell us more than any other source can about the kind of silverware used and the practices surrounding the Great Cover at the banquets given at the court of Louis XIV, for no illustrations have survived of the objects used and the customs followed at table in the French court in the seventeenth and eighteenth centuries. The picture reproduced here of the young Gustavus III at table with his family may help us understand what went on at other places besides Versailles, wherever courts were inspired by France.

A great damask linen cloth reaching down to the ground is spread over a square table; the artist has even reproduced the regular marks of very careful ironing! Gustavus III and the queen mother, Luise Ulrike of Prussia, are presiding at table. The king's two brothers are seated next to him and the young queen and the king's sister are beside the queen mother. The members of the court

26 Great Cover of King Gustavus III of Sweden and his family, Stockholm,
New Year 1773. Drottningholm Castle, Sweden. D 4535.

are either sitting on stools or standing around the table, according
to the rank associated with their functions at this public meal.

1773 was the year in which the Swedish Royal Academy was
founded. Gustavus III was ardent in his promotion of French
culture in his country, and it is not by chance that all the silverware
set out on this royal table is made in accordance with the latest
fashion in Paris, where rocaille work with all its excesses was
vehemently rejected and a return to the classical style strongly
favoured. Cochin's instructions were, after all, addressed primarily
to gold- and silversmiths.

Turning to the decoration of the table itself, we see in the centre
a runner made of mirrors and delicately framed with a silver gallery.
Both the little ceramic figures adorning it and the light from the
chandeliers and candlesticks are reflected in these mirrors. There

are neo-classical silver candlesticks around the edge of the table and
branched candelabra of the same type illuminate the centre of the
table. Two large tureens form part of the same service. One of
these, which is still covered, is placed in front of the king. The other
is uncovered and the ladle with a curved handle that can be seen
emerging from the top indicates that it must be a soup-tureen. Both
in shape and decoration these tureens recall the models that were
being produced at this time by Paris silversmiths for the Russian
court. The neo-classical style in silverware was extremely popular
in the Baltic countries then and later.

Plates of food are being brought to the diners, whose places are
set in accordance with contemporary custom, that is, with the knife
and the fork placed on either side of the plate and the spoon laid
horizontally above it. Bread is placed on a plate at the right-hand
side of each setting, and there is also a square covered box for salt
and pepper. The fork had apparently not yet been generally adopted
in Sweden even at this late date. This is clear from the fact that,

although the queen mother is using a fork, one of the princes still prefers to use his fingers. For some decades this habit had come in for widespread disapproval and it was certainly disappearing. The presence of soup-tureens on the table indicates that the meal was just beginning. This explains the absence of glasses, for drinking was not permitted at this stage. As we would expect, no glasses, decanters or coasters appear on the royal table.

This meal took place towards the end of the eighteenth century, when the art of table decoration and ceremonial had reached a peak of perfection never attained before. A new enthusiasm for large pieces of table silverware was gradually replacing the fashion for complete sets of china-ware that had dominated the first half of the century. Silver is far more easily adapted than earthenware to strictly neo-classical shapes, delicate columns and ornamentation. Even the political upheavals at the end of the century did not put an end to the general popularity of silver in preference to porcelain and china, on whose form and design it exerted increasing influence.

A Banquet in the Tuileries on the Occasion of the Marriage between Napoleon I and the Archduchess Marie Louise, 1810

Napoleon was most anxious to imitate and, if possible, to surpass the etiquette of the French royal court in magnificence and refinement. He therefore requested those responsible for arranging the ceremonies surrounding his marriage with Marie Louise of Austria in 1810 to draw on the record of feasts organized during the last years of the monarchy. He believed that his marriage would set the seal on his acceptance by the royal families of Europe and for that reason should be celebrated with unparalleled brilliance. He also wanted the memory of the occasion preserved for posterity in a series of paintings. I have chosen the picture of the imperial banquet mainly because it illustrates so well the development of table silverware under the Empire.

The great picture portraying this memorable feast, held on the stage of the theatre in the Palace of the Tuileries in Paris, certainly reveals how much the organizers owed to their model of forty years before. By an irony of fate Napoleon's wedding banquet was directly based on a group of feasts given at the Versailles Opera for the marriage between an aunt of Napoleon's bride and the Dauphin, the future Louis XVI. The setting of the banquet held in 1810 reflects the ambiguity of the situation, which also struck many observers at the time. On one hand Napoleon wanted to follow the traditions of the monarchy as faithfully as possible. On the other he did not recognize that the keynote of the magnificence of the court's table arrangements was simplicity. He set no limit to the lavish display of wealth that his organizers and their craftsmen wanted to create, with the result that he exposed himself to ridicule among the ancient aristocracy of Europe. His example was followed by almost every rich family in the nineteenth century, when tables were overloaded with silverware.

The table is set in a semi-circle on the stage of the palace theatre so that members of the court, who are present in the boxes, should have an excellent view of the spectacle. The table itself is concave in shape. It is covered with a white cloth fringed with gold and is almost collapsing under the weight of a monumental decoration consisting mainly of ostentatious silver objects. These articles certainly fulfil all the demands made by traditional royal etiquette, but appear to have lost their original function entirely. There are so many of them and they are so large and excessive that they can only be showpieces. For example, a little table is joined to each end of the main table, and each of these bears a huge silver-gilt nef, embossed with a monogram. The one on the Emperor's side has his monogram and the one on the Empress's side hers. Nefs were, of course, originally intended to hold the prince's cutlery, bread, salt and serviette, but these two nefs are clearly too far away from Napoleon and Marie Louise for them to be used for this purpose.

Only the married couple can be seen by the court. They are seated in the centre of the table. The massive and ostentatious decoration on either side almost completely hides the other diners, the members of the imperial family. This decoration consists of a broken table-runner formed of seven mirrors enclosed within a silver-gilt gallery and following the curve of the table. There is an empty centrepiece in the central mirror opposite the Emperor and Empress. Great china figures, placed at regular intervals, decorate the other parts of the table-runner. At each end of the central part of the table is a monumental silver-gilt *torchère*, or ornamental lampstand, with a round base. These *torchères* are surmounted by winged genies holding branches of light. They form a frame around the great ceramic candelabrum. Similar silver-gilt *torchères* appear at the end of a series of white china vases full of flowers. A combination of silver-gilt and china-ware, presumably of this kind,

27 Feast given on the stage of the theatre in the Tuileries, Paris, 1810, to ▷ celebrate the marriage between Napoleon I and the Archduchess Marie Louise of Austria. Painting by Casanova. Musée de Versailles.

was strikingly successful in 1770, when a banquet was held in the Opera at Versailles to celebrate the wedding of Louis XVI.

A row of silver-gilt cups and bowls containing fruit and delicacies can be seen between this monumental table-runner and the individual place settings. Beside each of the sovereigns' places, breaking this row of vessels, there is also a container for personal utensils or cadenas. This was, of course, traditionally placed beside the monarch at an earlier period, but hardly ever beside his wife, as we see here. These cadenas are superfluous on this table, in view of the presence of nefs. After all, the nef is an earlier and more monumental version of this container and the two never appeared together, as they do here.

The individual place settings consist of silver-gilt plates and high-quality knives, forks and spoons. It is, however, amusing to recall that, even at the Emperor's table, it was not regarded as wrong to eat with one's fingers! There is one great innovation on this table, which may have been introduced in order to emphasize the important achievements of the French cut-glass industry. Not every place at this table has a glass, but there are decanters holding wine and water in front of each diner. The servants are pouring drinks into the glasses of those guests who hold them out or else offering them glasses and decanters on silver-gilt coasters. Later glasses would form part of every place setting, increasing the brilliant effect of the table as a whole.

The Banquet of the Three Monarchs, London, 1814

It is very difficult to find reliable information about the way in which tables were arranged in England in the seventeenth and eighteenth centuries, but fortunately several excellent paintings from the first half of the nineteenth century show in minute detail the decoration of the splendid tables of this period, noted both for the quality and for the quantity of its silverware.

The banquet given in 1814 by the guilds of the City of London in honour of the Prince Regent, the Tsar and the King of Prussia to celebrate the Allies' victory over Napoleon has been recorded for posterity in George Clint's delightful painting. The artist has tried to reproduce all the details of the meal and this makes the picture valuable in our context, despite its rather mediocre quality.

The meal was held in the huge banqueting-room of the Guildhall, which was laid out to accommodate a large number of guests. The three monarchs can be seen sitting at the raised table at the back of the hall. Three long tables are placed at right angles to this high

table, almost adjoining it at its ends and its centre. The distinguished guests invited to the feast are seated on both sides of these three tables. Those allowed to watch the impressive spectacle do so from boxes in the upper part of the hall. Napoleon was largely blamed by his contemporaries in the rest of Europe for the taste for ostentation current in this period, but the same phenomenon existed in England as well, for the Prince Regent, the future King George IV, was also prone to this failing. During the Regency tables came to be decorated in a way that ran completely counter to the sober English tradition. The banquet of 1814 exemplifies his taste for lavish display.

The table at which the monarchs are seated is, as it should be, open to everybody's gaze. The rich decoration is dominated by a huge gilded table-runner. Its foundation consists of mirrors, on which are placed impressive candelabra of varying design. There are also old-fashioned trivets bearing baskets of fruit, great cups, and pillar candlesticks with many branches. Sweetmeat- or comfit-dishes are placed between these monumental silver-gilt objects. The only relatively empty space on the table is in front of the monarchs, who had to be in clear view of all the guests. Salt-cellars, pepper-casters and other spice-boxes are, however, scattered on the table at this point. The tallest articles in front of the three monarchs are great goblets with stems and dishes holding fruit. The development of table etiquette that occurred at the beginning of the century meant that the individual places now had to be set in a complicated way. The one that can be seen most clearly on the main table conforms to the English pattern and is composed of silver-gilt plates and matching dessert knives and forks. Opposite each place are wine and water decanters standing in their coasters, which have pierced silver-gilt vertical galleries and wooden bases. There are three glasses of different sizes, all belonging to the same set, in front of each place. The introduction of decanters and later of glasses was a great innovation. Large wine-coolers in the form of classical urns are set out at regular intervals along the table.

The decoration of the three tables in the foreground, at right angles to the main table, is much simpler. The objects on them are not of silver-gilt, but of plain silver. As the guests are seated on both sides of all three tables, there are no tall centrepieces or monumental lights to obstruct their view of each other. The table in the middle is decorated with a number of silver baskets of fruit standing on a foundation of mirrors. A table-runner consisting of mirrors

28 Banquet given for the Emperor of Russia, the King of Prussia and the Prince ▷
Regent of England in the London Guildhall, 1814. Painting by George Clint
(1770-1854). Guildhall Art Gallery, London.

enclosed within a silver gallery is laid along each side. There are also wine-coolers based on a classical design of the kind frequently produced by the well-known English silversmith, Paul Storr. Round cups containing fruit and delicacies are set out along the table-runner. The individual places consist of silver plates with elaborately worked inner edges, knives and forks, salts set on stands and a large number of glasses. The artist was so concerned with detail that he even reproduced the themes decorating the damask linen table-cloth, the ends of which are knotted. The taste for monumental table decorations evident here was to increase in the years that followed this banquet.

Banquets in the Waterloo Chamber of Apsley House, London, *c.* 1836

After the final victory over Napoleon at the battle of Waterloo in 1815, the Duke of Wellington used to invite all the heroes of the battle to a great annual banquet in his London residence, Apsley

29 Banquet held to commemorate the victory of Waterloo in 1836. Print by William Greatbach, based on painting by William Salter. Wellington Museum, Apsley House, London. AP 53.

30 *The Homage of the Nations Rendered to Victory.* Detail of centrepiece by the Portuguese silversmith, Domingos Antonio de Sequeira, and given to the Duke of Wellington by the Prince Regent of Portugal. This centrepiece traditionally decorated the table at the annual banquets held at Apsley House, London to commemorate the battle of Waterloo. Wellington Museum, Apsley House, London. AP 46.

31 The banqueting-hall used for the annual Waterloo Banquet at Apsley House, ▷ London, c. 1830. Water-colour by John Nash. Private collection.

House. Several paintings were made of these annual reunions, and are of interest to us here. The first one I have chosen is a reproduction of a great picture illustrating the banquet that took place in 1836. The second is a delightful water-colour by the architect John Nash. He was asked by the duke to arrange the immense banqueting-table and clearly thought it interesting enough to include in a collection of water-colours he made featuring different rooms in the house.

The artist who painted the first picture, William Salter (1804-75), sought to produce on one canvas portraits of all the heroes gathered around the table, in the manner of the great seventeenth-century Dutch compositions. He gives a very faithful rendering of these men, and also reproduces with great attention to detail the decoration of the table, two-thirds of which can be seen here.

Wellington himself can be easily picked out standing in the middle and addressing his guests. The huge table is covered with white cloths which hide the complex structure. The latter incorporates two monumental bronze candelabra, the bases of which are concealed beneath the table covering. These provide plenty of light at either end of the table. The whole central part is taken up by a magnificent centrepiece designed by the Portuguese silversmith Domingos Antonio de Sequeira in honour of the victory over Napoleon and given to the duke by the Prince Regent of Portugal.

The decoration of this table is very remote from the type of setting in which small-scale reproductions of monumental sculptures were used. The only real link with these eighteenth-century arrangements is the employment in both of silver. Its ability to reflect candle-light was obviously still greatly valued and this table clearly depended on silver for its splendid effect. There is also a great runner stretching almost the entire length of the table, edged with figurines holding garlands and branches of light. The centrepiece, however, is purely decorative and contains no functional object of any kind. The places laid for the guests, together with the glasses and decanters that went with them at this period, have little decorative value compared with the monumental central arrangement, so that the artist was not interested in them.

Turning now to Nash's water-colour, it is not difficult to detect a resemblance between the table decoration here and Salter's representation. Nash's picture, however, has the advantage of showing us the arrangement of the whole room before the guests arrived. It affords additional information about the silverware used for the banquet and reveals that there are flowers on the table. This must have been one of the first occasions when they appeared as a table decoration since the practice ceased at the beginning of the

seventeenth century. Attempts were made at the end of the Louis XV's reign to combine flowers with silver-plate in short-lived displays on the table and on silver sideboards, but they were quite rare. Here, probably for the first time, the ends of the table are adorned with great gilded vases containing climbing rose-plants with white flowers set against a background of moss. On each side of the dressers along the walls are more enormous urns full of flowers. A few years later these hesitant beginnings in floral decoration of the table would have become so firmly established that tables resembled greenhouses, with such a luxuriant abundance of flowers that there was hardly any room for the silverware.

The superb Portuguese centrepiece, resplendent with its bright gilding, can easily be seen standing between the huge bronze candelabra. Each place consists of a plate, hidden beneath a simply folded serviette, and on either side a battery of knives, forks and spoons. Each place is set out in the so-called 'Russian' manner, that is, according to the order in which the dishes are to be served. This was now generally replacing the traditional 'French' way of setting places. It will also be observed from Nash's water-colour that there are no dishes on the table. All courses were served by waiters in the order set down in the menu. The glasses and carafes appear alongside individual salt-cellars above the plates at each place.

All the silver required during the meal can be seen on four long dressers placed against the walls of the banqueting-hall.

This way of setting tables was decorative and artistic; it was also infinitely more economical and practical than previous table arrangements. As a result, once it had been perfected by the beginning of the nineteenth century, it developed very little. Even a hundred and fifty years after these banquets at Apsley House, meals of this magnificent kind continue to be served according to the conventions established in England at that time.

A Meal at the Townhouse of Princess Mathilde in the Rue de Courcelles, Paris, 1854

Although so much is known about everyday life in the nineteenth century, we have, strangely enough, been left almost completely in the dark about the way in which ordinary tables were decorated

32 The dining-room in the townhouse of Princess Mathilde in the Rue de ▷ Courcelles, Paris, 1854. Detail of painting by S.-C. Giraud. Musée National du Château, Compiègne.

with silverware. Fortunately, we do have descriptions which provide information about the more ostentatious meals given by great nineteenth-century hosts. We know, for example, that Talleyrand was the only person in the early nineteenth century to invite guests to banquets at tables adorned in the eighteenth-century manner and that no table was as superb as Baron Rothschild's.

The picture painted by C. Giraud in 1854 gives us a very good insight into the dining-room of one of the most prominent hostesses under the Second Empire. Princess Mathilde's Paris townhouse in the Rue de Courcelles must have been one of the most comfortable and luxurious dwellings of the period. The princess was also one of the few people to remain faithful to the French way of serving at table. This is all the more remarkable in view of the fact that, although the lunch illustrated here conforms to traditional table etiquette, only eleven places are set around the oval table. Was the Princess's apparent faithfulness to an outdated form of service really an attempt to ensure that the meal would proceed perfectly with the fewest servants at table, thus reducing the number of long ears present? In fact, the table setting in our illustration is a skilful blend of ancient and modern.

Princess Mathilde is shown accompanied by a sprightly officer in a 'Pompeian-style' dining-room, decorated in the best possible taste. She is receiving her guests, whom she has invited to share an intimate meal. They are arriving in procession and sitting down in comfortable seats upholstered in red velvet. There is a profusion of flowers, arranged as a winter-garden along the walls of the room. They have the appearance of a display of flowers in a carefully tended greenhouse. There are, however, no flowers at all on the table, which is covered with a neat white cloth.

A centrepiece might be placed on the table when the dessert was served, but at this stage its place is taken by a set of impressive round silver dishes with lamps beneath them. Their great shining covers are hemispherical in shape, with finials in the form of imperial eagles—Princess Mathilde was, after all, a close cousin of the Emperor Napoleon III. The plates and the bread lying on them are concealed beneath large, simply folded napkins. There is only one plate at each place, with the cutlery for the first course only on either side. These requisites are replaced as the course changes. At this time it was only in England that a whole battery of knives, forks and spoons, one set for each course, was displayed at each place. Later, when this practice was adopted in France, it was still not fully accepted. One concession to modern customs can, however, be seen on this table: glasses form part of the individual settings, positioned above the plates. The guests were able to serve

themselves as they pleased with wine and water, which were readily available in carafes between the place settings. The decorative salt no longer played any part in table arrangements and the merely functional salt-cellars are placed discreetly on the table.

Everything necessary for smooth service of the meal is prepared on a dresser at the end of the dining-room, where a servant can be seen at work. Silver plates from the piles on this dresser replace those already used at table. There are also several oil-cruets on the dresser and a centrepiece, which might be placed on the table when the dessert is served.

This meal, which took place in a fashionable townhouse in Paris in the mid-nineteenth century, is unpretentious, but undoubtedly very elegant in the most traditional sense. It is also my last example of a table adorned with that silver table-ware which formed the bulk of the silversmiths' output, at least until our present enthusiasm for early silver led us to try to find out exactly how so many silver objects, which seem to be so far removed from ordinary life, were in fact used.

Queen Charlotte of England at her Toilet, 1764

Silver toilet articles were in everyday use by men and women of rank. It is therefore not inappropriate to conclude this part of the book with a view of such silverware, especially as the toilet, like the meal, was governed by carefully regulated ceremonial. In Europe the queen's toilet was often the most important time of the day, when the most favoured members of the court were present.

In such circumstances it is hardly surprising that wealthy people of rank tried to have as many valuable silver objects as possible around them. From the seventeenth century onwards, the toilet- or dressing-table became a counterpart to the silver sideboard or buffet. It was used to display a large number of objects which had originally been functional, but which had gradually become purely ostentatious. By the eighteenth century the toilet-table, like the silver sideboard, had become a monument on which silver articles were exhibited but hardly ever touched, because they were too precious. People actually dressed and got ready for the public in an adjacent chamber, at a more comfortable table—and in privacy, far from indiscreet eyes. Those to whom special favour had been

33   Queen Charlotte at her dressing-table. Detail of portrait by Johann Zoffany ▷ (1733-1810), 1764. Her Majesty the Queen's Collection.

accorded were received only when finishing touches were being made at the dressing-table bearing the display of silver.

An eighteenth-century toilet-service normally consisted of a number of costly silver articles, most of which would have been given to the lady in question as part of her trousseau or even her dowry when she married. It was therefore never used but simply displayed in one's chamber on a table set aside for the purpose. Ladies in high society often had their portraits painted seated beside this exhibition of silver because this drew attention to their personal fortune in an even more emphatic way than their personal appearance or fine clothing.

This is certainly the impression given by the painting of the young Queen of England, Charlotte of Mecklenburg, and her two older sons, seen here at her toilet. This picture, painted by Johann Zoffany in the queen's chamber in Buckingham House in 1764, is not only quite delightful—it also tells us a great deal about her toilet-service.

The sovereign's apartment is unpretentious and the splendid silverware is set off to great advantage against this modest background. The table on which the various articles are arranged is richly adorned with Flemish lace. According to the court inventories, this was purchased only two years before the picture was painted. A covering, of the same Flemish lace, was hung over the great silver-gilt mirror, kept in place at the top by a great pink ribbon. If the two side fastenings were untied, the cover could be draped over the whole toilet-table, which would then be hidden beneath a pyramid of lace.

The silver-gilt toilet articles do not seem to have been made in England. They probably originated in Augsburg and formed part of the dowry of the young sovereign, who came from Strelitz. Among them are many finely worked objects in the distinctive style of the Augsburg craftsmen, who at that time enjoyed a virtual monopoly in Europe in the production of superb toilet-services. The great mirror is surrounded by a beautiful but quite sober silver-gilt frame with a simple convoluted moulding and without excessive ornamentation; in front of it is a bowl with lugs.

The viewer is not at first taken aback by the presence of this bowl but, on reflection, will realize that the queen is taking her lunch during the long preparation before her appearance in public. That is why it is not uncommon to find depicted in paintings such articles as coffee- or chocolate-pots, or cups and saucers, since drinks were frequently served to a lady's visitors. This particular soup-bowl, reproduced in great detail, corresponds almost exactly to a type fashionable in Germany throughout the eighteenth century. It is interesting to see that its cover has little feet in the form of volutes; turned over, it can be used as a plate or cup for left-overs.

On either side of the mirror are cut-glass scent-bottles with gold stoppers and a large square jewel-case. The lid of this casket is a pin cushion of red padded velvet. A lot of pins were used when dressing in the eighteenth century. Next to a pair of candlesticks are a large, richly embossed bowl, an oval covered box containing hair powder, and a smaller, star-shaped box with a circular handle for unguents and cosmetics. A ewer and basin are half hidden under the lace hangings. This was certainly the most important article in the whole toilet-set, but it was in no way different from the ewers and basins used at table. The many-foiled box with pierced decoration may have been a soap-container.

There were even more elaborate toilet-services, especially during the First Empire period, but the way in which the articles were arranged differed only slightly. This painting by Zoffany shows how silversmiths specializing in this kind of work were able to express themselves very freely. In wealthy homes the dressing-table with its toilet articles had the same decorative effect as the silver sideboard or the dining-table laid with silverware.

Part III

A Typology of Silver Objects

The Table

Drinking Vessels

The Goblet and Beaker

The goblet and beaker are as a rule the simplest precious metal objects and also the most widespread. Gold and silver goblets and beakers have been found earlier in history than almost any other precious object. Despite their obvious simplicity, they have been characterized at certain periods by a great diversity of shapes and sizes and by an almost infinite variety of decoration. This has, of course, changed according to fashion. The different types of goblet or beaker produced in each country, or even town, can be identified and dated without too much difficulty on the basis of these

characteristics. Because of their limited size and weight, and because they have a useful function, fewer goblets or beakers have been consigned to the melting-pot than other silver objects. Fortunately, there are enough of them for us to form a precise idea of the different types over the ages.

The simplest form of goblet is made by beating a circular sheet of metal into a hemispherical cup shaped like a drum or tympanum (hence the name). This type is found at almost every period, especially in France, Hungary and Germany. Closely related to this type is the beaker, which is cylindrical in shape, sometimes everted at the lip and closed at the bottom with a round plate of metal. There are many varieties based on one or other of these two prototypes and they have been produced wherever precious metals

34 Little goblet with a foot decorated with arabesques, Nuremberg or Strasbourg, mid-16th century. No hallmarks. Private collection.

35 Russian goblet or *bratina*, mid-17th century. Walters Art Gallery, Baltimore. 57.814.

36 Romer cup, Nuremberg, late 17th century, by an unidentified master with the initials HN. Private collection.

37 Covered goblet used as a case for a set of eating utensils, Augsburg, 1685/95, by Tobias Bauer, master silversmith 1685-1735. Private collection.

38 Great cup of brotherhood, Russia, mid-17th century. Walters Art Gallery, Baltimore. 57.794.

39

40

39 Beaker, Bienne, Switzerland, 1685, by Peter Rother (d. 1732). Private collection.

40 Covered beaker or cream container of silver gilt, Neuchâtel, *c.* 1700, by Nicolas Matthey, master silversmith 1670-1723. Private collection.

41 Covered beaker on three ball feet, entirely covered with filigree-work, Stockholm, 1691, by Ferdinand Sehl Sr. Nordiska Museet, Stockholm.

42 Tympanum-shaped beaker, turned over, Augsburg, *c.* 1710, by Johann Christoph I Hünning, master silversmith 1699-1737. Private collection.

41

42

43 Beaker shaped like a tympanum, Paris, 1713/14, by an unknown master. Metropolitan Museum of Art, New York. (Bequest of Catherine D. Wentworth, 1948.) 48.187.312.

44 Oval silver-gilt beaker decorated with rocaille-work, Dresden, 1759, by an unidentified master with the initials GM. Private collection.

have been available. Gold or silver have always been preferred for drinking vessels because it has been generally recognized that they are more hygienic materials. As there is clearly a limited number of basic forms, the place and date of origin are usually determined from the decoration, however simple.

At the period with which we are concerned, silver was frequently used for goblets and beakers in northern Europe, whereas in the south glass was preferred. In its simpler forms, glassware often imitated the more common types of goblet. In the seventeenth century, however, the reverse process took place and many goblets with stems were made in the graceful shapes of blown or cut-glass prototypes.

From the fifteenth century onwards silver beakers are frequently found in those parts of Europe where beer is drunk. This includes

the Low Countries which until the eighteenth century were extremely wealthy. Silver beakers here were made with great care and often in very large sizes, whereas they were almost always small in countries where they were used simply to hold water. Dutch and Flemish beakers are tall and cylindrical, widening out at the top. Some are made of plain silver; others are partly or entirely gilded. Frequently they bear engravings by the great masters, who also launched the art of engraving on paper.

Beakers were exported in great numbers from the Low Countries, especially to England, the cities of the Hanseatic League and the Scandinavian towns, where Dutch and Flemish people had many trading contacts. Their beakers were also frequently copied in northern European countries. There were even more obvious trade links with the Rhineland and southern Germany. Such beakers

45 Set of six little nesting goblets for brandy, partly covered with niello, Moscow, 1765, by Georg Ritmeier, master silversmith 1773-5. Private collection.

They were frequently decorated in relief and on a flat surface. In the seventeenth century they were sometimes discreetly given matted surfaces up to the neck or else bore floral designs or scrolls of foliage in relief. Many excellent goblets and beakers were produced in Nuremberg, Augsburg and various Swiss towns during that century. Then and later Strasbourg was a very important centre of the European silver industry. Craftsmen here were subjected to both French and German influence. In the eighteenth century silversmiths in Strasbourg made exquisite goblets shaped like tulips, a type that became the most popular in France. In Paris they were often covered with a decoration from the classical repertory of gadrooning and foliage.

German centres of silver production such as Augsburg and Dresden made goblets and beakers in more contorted shapes in the eighteenth century. Their ware was elegantly cut and shaped and accorded with the contemporary taste for rocaille work. The nineteenth century was the age of blown and cut glass, and the silver goblet or beaker almost completely disappeared from the scene. It came to be used mainly by children, so that its shape naturally became much simpler.

were popular wherever a great deal of beer was consumed, partly because it was usual to drink warm or at least lukewarm beer and it cooled down less quickly in silver beakers than in glasses, as we noted when considering table-ware used in seventeenth-century Zurich.

Beakers produced in Sweden, Norway and Russia can be distinguished quite easily by their decorative details. Traditional forms and ornamentation were faithfully preserved much longer in these parts of Europe than elsewhere. At the turn of the seventeenth and eighteenth centuries a trumpet-shaped beaker, very wide at the top, made its appearance. In the eighteenth century extra-large drinking vessels tended to disappear as French influence spread, but the earlier tradition persisted in Russia, where a type made of silver-gilt, lavishly decorated with rocaille work and niello, evolved.

Smaller goblets or beakers were more popular in Germany and Switzerland, where both wine and beer have always been drunk. In the sixteenth and seventeenth centuries sets of as many as eight or twelve identical vessels were frequently produced. Such sets might be displayed together with hanaps on silver sideboards, sometimes stacked in a pyramid and sometimes inserted one inside the other with a finely wrought cover on top, in the manner discussed above. At that time goblets were rather squat and often had short stems.

The Hanap

The word 'hanap' is used for many different kinds of drinking vessel that are larger and more impressively worked than goblets or beakers. Hanaps are above all ceremonial objects and were never used in everyday life. Throughout the Middle Ages they were reserved exclusively for sovereigns, but in the sixteenth century, when there was a fall in the price of silver, their use became much wider in Protestant countries. As we noted when discussing the table-ware of the Faesch family of Basle, after losing their most important customer, the Church, silversmiths were obliged to produce objects for civil purposes. It would not be wrong to call

46 Large hanap in form of a bunch of grapes, surmounted by a figure of Hope, Nuremberg, c. 1540, by Jörg Ullrich. Private collection.

47 Double "Willkomm" hanap with the coats of arms of the town of Schaffhausen and the Convent of Allerheiligen, Nuremberg (?), c. 1540. No hallmarks. Private collection.

48 Double hanap, belonging to General de Pfyffer d'Altishofen (1524-94). A gift by Charles IX, King of France, to the General of the Swiss Guard, Paris, 1567, by Denis Roussel, master silversmith (before 1541, d. before 1581). One half of this hanap is in a private collection; the other half is in the Swiss National Museum, Zurich. LM 666.

46

47

48

51 Hanap in the form of a snail carried by a satyr, Augsburg, 1567-85, by a master belonging to the Hueter family of silversmiths. Swiss National Museum, Zurich. 2855.

52 Heraldic hanap in form of an ibex, Augsburg, *c.* 1620, by Balthasar I Lerff, master silversmith 1602-22. Private collection.

53 Hanap in the form of a lion holding a tanner's knife, Augsburg, 1630/45, by Georg I Lotter, master silversmith *c.* 1618-61. Swiss National Museum, Zurich. 2896.

54 Heraldic hanap in form of a fair-ground bear, Augsburg, 1674, by Marx Merzenbach, master silversmith 1642-88. Private collection.

49-50 Double hanap that can be used as small goblets and a candlestick, Nuremberg, *c.* 1580, by Jost Heberle, master silversmith in 1575, mentioned until 1586. Private collection.

51

52

53

54

55 Heraldic hanap in the form of a cock, belonging to the Blarer family, Augsburg, *c.* 1685-96, by Matthäus or Markus Wolff, master silversmith 1685-1716. Swiss National Museum, Zurich. LM 11044.

56 Design for a hanap featuring King Gustavus Adolphus II of Sweden on his horse, attributed to Hans Friedrich Schorer of Augsburg, *c.* 1630. Nationalmuseet, Stockholm. NMH 243/1931.

hanaps secular counterparts of sacred vessels. There are many similarities between the two types of silverware.

The great age of hanaps was confined to the sixteenth and seventeenth centuries, although there was a certain revival in the nineteenth century. They were made almost exclusively in northern Europe and for very much the same reasons as goblets and beakers. The hanap is in fact a monumental goblet. It allows the silversmith to demonstrate his inventiveness and it is hardly surprising that all the great specialists in artistic decoration at the time provided silversmiths with very imaginative designs. Dürer, Holbein and their successors down to Stefano della Bella and Adam van Vianen

produced a great number of extraordinary drawings for such vessels.

The taste for hanaps of unusual shape and design probably originated in Antwerp at the time of the dukes of Burgundy. The sixteenth-century religious wars forced many Protestant silversmiths to leave Flanders and France and to seek refuge in Nuremberg. Since the end of the fifteenth century the craftsmen of this city had been specializing in a technique of silver-work that was extremely fine and lightweight. By the beginning of the sixteenth century they were producing major works of art whose shapes and decorative themes had a pronounced influence on architecture and

57 Goblet in the form of a lady in full dress. The skirt could be used as a cup. Zurich, late 16th century, by an unidentified master. Musée du Louvre, Paris. OA 629/MV 352.

58 Stemmed cup, London, c. 1612, by H. Barington. Museum of Fine Arts, Boston. (Theodora Wilbour Fund.) 62.167.

59 Stemmed cup of silver-gilt, Basle, c. 1640, by Isaak Schilling, master silversmith 1627-55. Private collection.

sculpture. The hanaps created in Nuremberg were not only sold but also copied in all the wealthiest towns of Europe. Craftsmen in Hamburg, for example, made hanaps in the style of those produced at Nuremberg and Augsburg and sold them in all the towns on the Baltic coast, even in Russia.

The Flemish and German Mannerists who specialized in silverware and the later Baroque craftsmen moved away from traditional forms and went to extremes of fantasy in their work, creating hanaps in human, animal and architectural shapes. Such vessels offered a pretext for decorating tables and sideboards with sculpture in silver. Hanaps were sometimes even transformed into

automata, since parts of them could be made to move by a complicated mechanism hidden in the base. The untranslatable German word for such objects, *Trinkspiel*, shows that they never penetrated into France or Italy, but many of these mechanized hanaps are masterly examples of the silversmith's art. In the Low Countries, for instance, they were made in the form of windmills on little hills, and became drinking vessels when they were turned. Little figurines with large skirts and other comical figures were used to entertain guests at banquets.

Hanaps in the form of tulips and other flowers, pineapples, bunches of grapes, pomegranates or similar fruit persisted from the fifteenth until the late seventeenth century in German-speaking countries. These forms gave silversmiths of Nuremberg, Augsburg, Ulm, Basle, Zurich and Berne a chance to demonstrate their skill. It can hardly be claimed, however, that these hanaps, which were really works of sculpture in precious metal, were intended for use as drinking vessels. It is difficult to imagine guests putting the neck of a decapitated Swiss mercenary to their lips and drinking the wine contained in his body, even if the statuette was of silver-gilt! Another speciality of Nuremberg and Augsburg craftsmen was a whole bestiary of lions, bears, wild goats, leopards, birds and other winged creatures. These countless heraldic animal hanaps can never have been used regularly for drinking. They were primarily decorative objects kept on the silver tables or sideboards of wealthy guild members in German and Swiss towns.

Cups with Stems

The basic form of these elegant drinking vessels is a large shallow bowl with a central stem, which tended to become longer in the course of time. The term most frequently used for this type of cup is tazza, which clearly points to its Italian origin. It was derived from a glass prototype and is an imitation in precious metal of one of the most graceful products of Venetian master craftsmen. The stemmed silver cup was popular in many European countries from the sixteenth to the early eighteenth century.

The first examples appeared in France at the court of Francis I and Henry II, where masters of the decorative arts of the Fontainebleau school, who were either Italian or directly influenced by Italian art, provided silversmiths with superb models on which to base their work. Almost all the products of this period have unfortunately disappeared. Antwerp silversmiths, however, also made early cups of this type, following the examples of the Fontainebleau school. So many objects were exported from

60 A tazza used to contain delicacies. Detail of picture by Clara Peeters (*c.* 1589-after 1617), Antwerp, *c.* 1600. Alte Pinakothek, Munich. 1524.

61 Tazza, probably Lisbon, late 16th century, by the master silversmith known ▷ as Andres. Private collection.

71

62 Tazza, Zurich, 1693, by Hans Jacob III Bullinger, master silversmith 1672-1724. Swiss National Museum, Zurich. 382.

63 A man drinking from a tazza. Detail of picture by Dirk Hals (1591-1656). National Gallery, London.

Antwerp at that time that stemmed cups can be found wherever merchants from that city travelled: the Hanseatic towns and indeed the whole of Germany, Switzerland, and even Spain, with which the Low Countries had close dynastic ties. Few such cups found their way to England, however, and none were taken to Italy, which remained faithful to traditional Venetian glass.

By the late sixteenth century Nuremberg had become an important centre of medal production and its silversmiths were already excelling those of Antwerp in mastery of their craft. They decorated the inside of the bowl with small and finely chased plates, following the plans of the best artists of the period. At the same time, craftsmen such as Abraham Gessner, who had links with Antwerp and the Low Countries, made Zurich another centre where cups with stems were produced.

The silversmith was always able to express his skill in ornament on the stem of these cups and frequently shaped it with the greatest care. On the bowl decoration was at first, in the sixteenth century, confined to the interior of the bowl; it was not until the following century that the outside was decorated as well. This was due to the fact that these cups were found less than satisfactory as vessels from which to drink wine, and so gradually became objects to be admired rather than used. This is clear from contemporary paintings, in which they are shown holding flowers, fruit or sweetmeats. The richly chased base of the bowl which made the wine sparkle was abandoned in favour of rich decorations sculpted in relief or engraved on the outer surface. The only cups with stems produced in the eighteenth century are those that can now be seen in the treasures belonging to the Swiss merchant guilds. They survived long enough in Switzerland to be revived in the nineteenth century as trophy cups.

72

The Wine-Cup

The round cup without a stem, wider at the mouth than at the base, is a form of wine goblet or beaker that goes back to the earliest period of human history and is still commonly found in almost every part of Europe. This type of cup, which is derived from the beaker, has a variety of shapes, but is almost always round. Sometimes it is found with two handles or lugs, but is never too big to be held in one hand. Many vessels of this kind are richly decorated, partly because repoussé chasing enables the silversmith to use less metal without making the cup unstable. The most common decoration is a cupulate one or else of cut diamonds, both of which make the wine sparkle attractively. It was regarded as a great advantage to employ less metal for a decorated cup during the Middle Ages, when silver was an extremely precious commodity. Almost the only silver articles used outside the Church that have miraculously survived until now are a few wine-cups. It is quite certain that this was then the most widespread form of drinking vessel among the wealthy.

In their palaces drink and food were carefully supervised by cup-bearers and other domestic staff. These servants were trusted by their masters, who were always exposed to the risk of poison. The cup-bearer would taste the mixture of wine and water in a wine-cup and then offer it to his master in a hanap. The 'assay cup' used for testing the wine and the hanap in which it was presented were often made together by the silversmith, the former serving as a cover for the latter. These double hanaps were very popular until the end of the sixteenth century and were among the most magnificent silver objects made at that time. The wine-cup with lugs was so common in the late Middle Ages that wine merchants adopted a smaller version of it for wine-tasting.

The Russian *kovsh* was evolved from this basic form of wine-cup. All the usual elements of the drinking vessel are present, but its shape is that of a little boat with a lug at one end to hold it by. The

64 Wine-cup, Nuremberg, *c.* 1610, by Heinrich Straub. Private collection.

65 Wine- or brandy-cup, Amsterdam, 1641, by J. Lutma. Rijksmuseum, Amsterdam.

kovsh, which can vary very greatly in size, is essentially a boat with a short handle. Its prototype was undoubtedly a cup carved out of wood. It is reputed to have been invented at Novgorod in the fourteenth century and may well have derived from the Western European form of wine-cup.

66   Russian cup or *kovsh*, Moscow, 1680, by an unidentified master. Walters Art Gallery, Baltimore. 57.798.

74

The Wine-Taster (*taste-vin*)

This word is probably derived from the classical French term *tasse à vin*, meaning wine-cup in the general sense. The expression *taste-vin* is now applied to the very small wine-cup used for sampling wine. The wine-taster is certainly the smallest drinking vessel of all and is found not only in the countries where wine is produced, but wherever wine is bought and sold. Wine-tasters exist in relatively large numbers, since the use of precious metal in their manufacture is a necessity rather than a luxury. They are in fact indispensable tools of the vintner's trade and are used to taste, smell and examine wine for clarity and appearance.

Wine-tasters of various shapes and with individual details evolved in different parts of Europe and collectors now look for them with special enthusiasm. There are very many examples in France. Until the late eighteenth century Bordeaux remained faithful to a kind of wine-taster that was most directly inspired by the ancient form of this vessel. It had a chased umbilicus in the centre of the bowl to make the wine sparkle, but was not decorated and had no handle. Silver wine-tasters by Norman craftsmen have a thumbplate on the rim. Although relatively rare, Burgundian wine-tasters are the most varied in form and the most richly worked. Such vessels are also found in the Low Countries and Switzerland, where fine examples were produced between the sixteenth and nineteenth century. They are less frequently encountered in Germany and are almost unknown in England or America.

Wine-tasters are often confused with bleeding-cups, but the latter are usually larger; they are also provided with ring-shaped handles, with or without a thumbplate, and convoluted handles or lugs, which may be either simple or pierced.

67   *The Guild of Wine-Merchants.* One of the members is emptying the contents of a silver wine-extractor into a wine-taster. Detail of painting by Ferdinand Bol (1616-80), *c.* 1660. Alte Pinakothek, Munich.

68   Wine-taster, France, 18th century. Metropolitan Museum of Art, New York. (Bequest of Catherine D. Wentworth, 1948.) 48.187.153.

Brandy-Cups

Cups of this kind, almost all of silver-gilt, were as common as goblets and beakers in those regions in which little or no wine but a great deal of brandy was drunk. They are sometimes known as marriage or loving cups and formed part of the marriage customs in most northern European lands, where it was usual for young couples to celebrate their commitment to each other by drinking brandy or similar spirits from a single cup. These brandy-cups are widespread, although their size and shape varies from country to country and from period to period. What they all have in common is a handle on either side.

The smallest cups are usually oval, with a flat base and a convoluted rim, which make these very light vessels more stable. Like the beaker, the brandy-cup was frequently found in quite unpretentious households. It appeared from the end of the sixteenth until the mid-eighteenth century in Germany, the Low Countries, Switzerland and the lands of central Europe. Often only the handles were decorated; they were sometimes shaped as caryatids, as in the sixteenth-century example made at Nuremberg. Floral themes are sometimes found on the inside of the base of the bowl and even on the sides.

These little cups were often also used for drinking soup and the brandy-cup can therefore legitimately be regarded as the prototype of the soup-bowl. This relationship is even more obvious when the very large brandy-cups made by Scandinavian silversmiths are taken into consideration. The Swedish *kåsa*, for example, which has two handles, one on each side, can be as large as a little soup-tureen, but it was used for drinking spirits.

69 Bowl with a lid that could be used as a plate, Copenhagen, 1687, by Mathias Hielm (?). Kunstindustrimuseet, Oslo. OK 7995.

The Tankard

A special form of drinking vessel, derived from the beaker, was invented in German-speaking countries in the sixteenth century for beer. This was drunk warm or lukewarm at that time, as we have mentioned. If this surprises us nowadays, we should remember that no other warm drink, such as tea, coffee or chocolate, was then known in Europe. It would be futile to look for tankards in such wine-drinking countries as France, Italy, Spain or Portugal. They have, however, been common for a long time in beer-drinking countries, both on the Continent and in the English-speaking world.

The tankard is not necessarily always made of silver. Some tankards are of quite unusual materials, such as wood, glass, horn, amber, porcelain, stone or ivory. Its shape is always the same, although the size may vary. It consists basically of a cylinder, which may or may not be wider at the top or bottom. It may have a base and almost always has a cover that is hinged at one side and a handle on that same side. These features show that the tankard occupied an intermediate position between the drinking vessel and the pot or jug.

Its shape and size were largely determined by local customs. This means that, even without the help of hallmarking, most tankards can be identified quite easily. They can also be dated with a high degree of precision, because their engraved or chased decoration always accords with contemporary taste. The disappearance of the tankard in the middle of the eighteenth century was due to the rising popularity of tea, coffee and chocolate, which tended to replace beer, especially as drinks for ladies.

However astonishing it may seem to us now, small tankards were used almost exclusively by ladies. Evidence of this practice, in southern Germany and Switzerland especially, can be found in many illustrations of the period. Husbands often gave their wives a tankard—as they sometimes also gave them a bowl—when the first child was born. This was because beer was thought to improve lactation. The fact that they were intended for women explains why they were so small, rather compact and richly decorated. From the sixteenth century onwards Augsburg was the leading centre, setting the fashion in form and decoration and influencing the way in which these objects were made in the south of Germany and Switzerland.

There is also another type of tankard, with a much greater capacity, which is taller and always has a large handle with a double curve. These larger tankards, which were fashionable from the sixteenth century onwards in the north of Germany and Europe generally, were less subject to variations and were almost exclu-

70 Tankard with coat of arms of the Supersaxo family. The end of a tube can be seen on the handle. One could suck the warm beverage through this tube without opening the tankard lid. Sion, late 16th century, by an unknown silversmith. Swiss National Museum, Zurich. LM 757.

77

71 A husband bringing a tankard as a present to his young wife in confinement. Detail of drawing by Jonas Arnold the Younger (1609-69), 1656. Kupferstichkabinett, Berlin (Staatliche Museen Preussischer Kulturbesitz).

72 Silver-gilt tankard with Jonas Arnold's drawing engraved on the body, Stuttgart, c. 1660, by Jeremias Peffenhauser. Württembergisches Landesmuseum. 1636/194.

73 Silver-gilt tankard, Lachen, Switzerland, 1699, by Johann Sebastian Gruber (1675-1742). Swiss National Museum, Zurich. LM 46999.

74 Large tankard, Stockholm, 1641, by Caspar Beck (?). Nordiska Museet, Stockholm.

75 Tankard engraved with chinoiserie themes, London, c. 1605. No maker's hallmarks. Museum of Fine Arts, Boston. (Theodora Wilbour Fund.) 20.2724.

sively used by men. Some tankards made in towns on the Baltic coast—Danzig, for example—and in Hanseatic cities such as Hamburg, where so many silver-gilt ones were produced in the seventeenth century, were enormous. These monuments in silver often found their way into the treasures of merchant guilds. Their handles are normally richly decorated; they sometimes have ball or voluted feet which are the only decorated parts, the barrel remaining undecorated.

The typical Danish and Norwegian tankards are mounted on three feet, usually in the form of balls or open pomegranates, sometimes shaped like human figures or animals. A favourite form was the heraldic lion couchant. The lids of Scandinavian tankards are always very flat, emphasizing their squat, compact appearance.

74

73   75

79

◁ 76   Tankard, England, *c.* 1670, by an unidentified master with the initials IB. Museum of Fine Arts, Boston. (Theodora Wilbour Fund.) 55.461.

The gilding of silver tankards differs according to their place of origin. The Germans and Swiss favoured vessels that were entirely of silver-gilt. Swedish tankards are gilded only on the inside and the rim. Danish and Norwegian ones are never gilded, nor are English and North American lidded tankards and mugs without lids. First imported from Germany and the Scandinavian countries about 1570, these tend to be very simple, partly because they were widely used in English and American society.

The English-speaking peoples alone remained faithful to the silver tankard until the present. The first tankards made in England were strongly influenced by the tall, slender North German models. They have feet and a moulded rib and are richly engraved. They have domed covers and their handles are always shaped. Until the mid-seventeenth century English tankards were closer to the Baltic prototype. From about 1620 onwards they often had very flat lids with impressive thumb-pieces, simple but quite wide handles ending in a little shield, and ball feet. Towards the end of the seventeenth century Protestant silversmiths from France influenced the English tankard by adding engravings on the barrel. The owner's coats of arms or initials or other forms of decoration were frequently engraved on English tankards, but these ornaments were always discreet in comparison with those found in German and Scandinavian countries or in Russia.

The citizens of East Prussian towns at this time liked the barrels of their tankards to be entirely covered with coins. These ostentatious articles were often extremely large and were kept on a silver sideboard rather than on the table. They were in striking contrast to the smaller models, which generally contained no more than a pint of beer. Until the eighteenth century the most graceful, varied and finely gilded tankards, based on French, Italian and German designs, were made in Augsburg and the south German towns.

Pouring-Vessels

Ewers

Individual places set with cutlery, and forks in particular, were not usual at meals until the seventeenth century and were certainly not generally accepted as an indispensable feature of the table arrange-

77   Ewer, Madrid, *c.* 1590, by José de Madrid. Victoria and Albert Museum, London.

ment until the first decades of the eighteenth century. Until then people mainly ate with their fingers and therefore needed to have water available to rinse them, not only at the beginning and end of every meal but also during it.

It hardly needs to be pointed out that ewers and similar vessels made of precious metal were confined to the homes of the wealthier members of society. Such vessels were not really indispensable and, because they were heavy, were always burdensome. For this reason they were often the first to be sent to the melting-pot when the family fortunes changed or the state imposed sumptuary laws.

Silver ewers are also quite rare now because table manners changed when forks came to be widely used. Moreover, Louis XIV introduced a fashion that was imitated throughout Europe. He preferred to wipe his hands with a wet napkin presented to him between two plates during and after the meal.

On the other hand, the ewer and basin were more suitable than any other object for display on silver buffets, and so silversmiths everywhere went on making them until the early nineteenth century. They always gave special attention to them, initially because of their important function at table.

In the sixteenth and seventeenth centuries Spain and Portugal had more gold and silver at their disposal than any other country because of their colonies in Latin America. This abundance of precious metal is not, however, the only explanation for the relatively large number of ewers and basins that have survived on the Iberian peninsula. It is rather the scarcity of water in that part of Europe that has resulted in their continued use. The traditional Spanish ewer is a massive vessel, shaped like an inverted helmet, with a low base and heavily ribbed body; it is frequently decorated with lions' snouts. Because ceramic art reached a peak of perfection in Moorish Spain that it achieved nowhere else in Europe, the silver ewer was usually based on porcelain prototypes. The same applies to the great round basins with a shallow central depression for the ewer to rest in.

Because of trade links with Antwerp and the Low Countries generally, Portuguese silverware was directly influenced by the work of Flemish silversmiths. Portuguese traders took colonial commodities that were eagerly sought in the Low Countries to Flemish ports and brought back richly decorated silver objects. To distinguish their work from that executed in the simpler Spanish style, Portuguese craftsmen adopted the opulent taste of Antwerp. Because of their size, ewers and basins could be decorated with scenes of figures, surrounded by different kinds of ornamentation. Despite its proximity to Portugal, Spain continued to favour the abstract decoration that it had inherited from its Islamic past. In the seventeenth century the only aspect of Flemish art to be adopted in Spain was a taste for the grotesque, which in fact originated in the Fontainebleau school. Later both Portugal and Spain, which had for so long differed from each other artistically, continued to be faithful to the style that had predominated during each country's golden age.

It was in Italy, where table settings with cutlery, including forks, napkins and so on were introduced earlier than elsewhere in Europe, that the ewer and basin first became objects for display. Freed from the restraints imposed by function, silversmiths chose shapes and adornments which would make their work admired. This decoration was often monumental, especially towards the end of the sixteenth century. Ewers with large oval bellies and narrow necks, based on models originally found in ancient works, tended to disappear. The newer, more richly adorned ewers were baluster-

78   Large silver-gilt water-jug, Spain, early 17th century. No hallmarks. Private collection.

79   Ewer with basin, Augsburg, *c.* 1720, by a silversmith of the Peffenhauser ▷ family. Private collection.

shaped and were always accompanied by round basins with a shallow central depression. Each important town evolved its own type, but the ewer and basin became a speciality of Genoese craftsmen from the sixteenth century onwards. They enjoyed a kind of monopoly in Italy until the end of the eighteenth century.

In the sixteenth century English silversmiths, who were at that time totally under Flemish and Spanish influence, made ewers in

heavy shapes, either richly decorated or else completely unadorned. From the beginning of the seventeenth century, however, they came to be more influenced by the very Italian style of van Vianen and other master-craftsmen from the Low Countries and from Italy itself. The two types of ewer, one shaped like a helmet placed upside-down and the baluster-shaped vessel, continued to exist side by side until the revocation of the Edict of Nantes led many

80 Jug at one end of the display of Louis XIV's gold and silverware. Detail of picture by François Desportes (1661-1743), c. 1700. Musée du Louvre, Paris. 3947.

81 Design for a ewer, Rome, c. 1700. Cooper-Hewitt Museum, New York. 1938-88-2485.

82 Design for a jug, Rome, late 17th century. Cooper-Hewitt Museum, New York. 1938-88-2139.

83 Ewer with arms of the King of Portugal, Paris, 1757/8, by François Thomas Germain, master silversmith 1748-91. Museu Nacional de Arte Antiga, Lisbon.

Huguenot silversmiths to seek refuge in England, where they soon made the inverted helmet shape the definitive and generally acccptcd form. As in France, the ewer and basin were used on the toilet-table or else displayed on the silver sideboard.

The ewer and basin did not appear in German-speaking countries until after the mid-sixteenth century. From then onwards, however, they became very popular. The basins, which were usually not round but oval, often gave the skilful Nuremberg

silversmiths an opportunity to add scenes of figures in bas-relief in the centre of a decorative composition. Augsburg craftsmen followed those of Nuremberg and took over their monopoly of the production of such vessels. Their versions were richly decorated but much lighter. About 1600 basins, now used more and more frequently at toilet-tables, became much deeper. Being fit both for the toilet and for display, they were sold in considerable quantities not only in Germany, but also in most other parts of Europe until the late eighteenth century. The silversmiths who made them adapted their designs to cater to the new French taste, basing the decoration on engravings and prints from all over Europe.

84 Water-jug with basin, Paris, 1727/9, by Léopold Antoine, master silversmith in 1706. Metropolitan Museum of Art, New York. (Bequest of Catherine D. Wentworth, 1948.) 48.187.21/22.

Although Augsburg ewers and basins found their way to almost every corner of Europe, French craftsmen, who at first had simply adopted the Spanish model and then the Italian one, developed a type of ewer and basin intended exclusively for toilet purposes. This occurred in the eighteenth century. Previously, Louis XIV's silversmiths had created monumental ewers and basins to match the monarch's silver furnishings, which will be discussed below.

85 Wine-jug, England, *c.* 1825. Private collection.

86 Wine-jug, Birmingham, 1776, by Matthew Boulton and John Fothergill. Museum of Fine Arts, Boston. (Theodora Wilbour Fund.) 55.623.

Pots, Jugs and Flasks

These vessels have always been used in a similar way to ewers, but it is worth describing them separately, as their evolution was different. Although pots and jugs were employed very widely in the Middle Ages and appear in many medieval illustrations, very few examples have survived. Small pouring-vessels, especially of the kind used by the Church, have been produced in as great a variety of forms as larger versions.

The silver pot with a long spout was based on the Turkish or Persian porcelain rose-water pourer and retains all the features of its Asian prototype, imitated in Europe above all because of its elegant shape. It originally had no special function and was used for pouring water, wine or any other drink. Venice, which had strong trading links with the Middle East, was the first European city in which the pot first appeared and also the only place where it retained its basic form for a long time. Eighteenth-century Venetian coffee-pots were based directly on the Asian original. At this time pots could be found wherever European art forms were influenced by Islam, notably in Spain, Sicily and Russia. Later, identical examples occur in south Germany and France.

87 Large silver-gilt pouring-vessel belonging to the kings of Portugal, early 18th century. No hallmarks. Private collection.

88 Silver flask, The Hague, 1680, by Adam Loots (?). Devonshire Collection, Chatsworth House, England.

89 *Aquamanile*, or pouring-vessel in shape of a lion, probably from Spain, early ▷ 16th century. No hallmarks. Private collection.

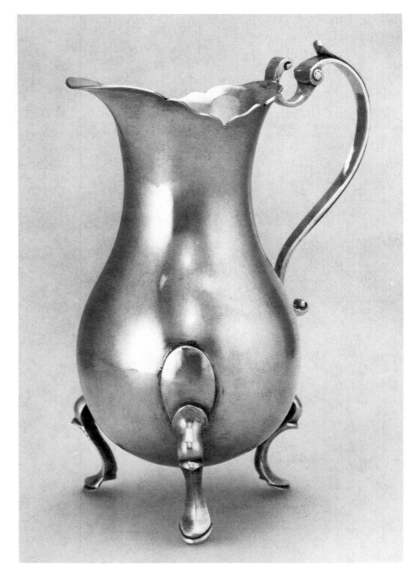

90 Wine-strainer, London, 1791/2, by B. Mountigue, master silversmith from 1772. Private collection.

91 Milk-jug with three feet, Basle, *c.* 1785, by Johann Friedrich I Burckhardt, master silversmith 1781-1827. Private collection.

In sixteenth-century England, on the other hand, a type of jug evolved out of the tall cylindrical tankard, which had itself been developed from the tankard produced in Hanseatic towns. Many huge silver jugs were made, only a few of which have survived; they can be seen in the Arsenal of the Moscow Kremlin.

In addition to these two types of pouring-vessel, which are the most common, there is a third type which is flask-shaped. The silver flask with chain is based on a common and very simple medieval object of practical use. It remained very popular until the end of the seventeenth century in Germany, England and France. The silver flask was the distinguishing mark, at the French court and at all others where the ceremonial was inspired by the French model, of the master cup-bearer, the functionary in charge of the wine, who alone had the task of opening and closing it. The flask was also adopted in Italy as a pouring-vessel, but here it was made of porcelain and never of silver. In Germany and Switzerland a miniature version of this vessel served as a scent-bottle from the late seventeenth to the late eighteenth century.

One object that has completely disappeared from the catalogue of domestic silverware is the great silver wine-fountain which figured so frequently in medieval and Renaissance royal treasures. Artists such as Dürer, Holbein and Jamnitzer drew models which were followed by the most skilful silversmiths of the period. These objects were still found at the Swedish court in the seventeenth century. It was at about this time that they were replaced on the table by centrepieces, which from then onwards were the principal item of decoration.

92 Little covered jug for warm milk, Scotland, *c.* 1750. No hallmarks. Private collection.

93 Large milk-jug in the shape of an inverted helmet, *c.* 1800. No hallmarks. Private collection.

The Tea-Pot

In the course of the seventeenth century the three so-called colonial drinks, tea, coffee and chocolate, were brought into Europe. This caused a revolution in drinking habits and fundamentally changed the work of silversmiths. In the first place they had to find new ways of selling pouring-vessels made especially for these new beverages. Secondly, they had to convert a great number of old goblets, beakers and hanaps that were now melted down into an array of silver articles that could be used to serve the new drinks.

The first dried tea-leaves were imported from China into the Netherlands in 1610. The Dutch East India Company, which was better organized than its competitors, was responsible for the country's wealth in the seventeenth century. Holland's prosperity aroused the envy of France, which conducted trade wars with

disastrous effect and adopted all the methods used by the Dutch in their dealings with the Far East.

Tea was at first regarded as a medicinal drink and was not immediately accepted in France, even though the Dutch East India Company introduced it in Paris in 1602 for this purpose. In the Low Countries it was initially drunk only by sailors, who in the course of their voyages in Asian waters had discovered that it was both toxic and stimulating. When they returned home, they began to drink tea for pleasure. This practice was regarded as indecent by the middle classes. Tea was absolutely forbidden in the salons and was thought to be a drink that no respectable lady should touch.

In Europe generally sailors were the first to drink tea. They prepared it in the way that they had seen it made in China, that is, by pouring boiling water on to tea-leaves in an earthenware or china dish or cup and drinking the infusion from the same cup or from the saucer. There is no evidence in Holland to suggest that tea was then

94

94 Tea-pot, London, 1686, by an unidentified master with the initials FSS. Museum of Fine Arts, Boston. (Theodora Wilbour Fund.) 1955.193.

95 Broth-pot, with spout, North America (Massachusetts), *c.* 1680, by Jeremiah Dummer (1645-1718). Museum of Fine Arts, Boston. (Gift of Mrs. Horatio A. Lamb.) 41.221.

96 Chocolate- or tea-pot, North America (Massachusetts), *c.* 1701, by John Coney (1655/6-1722). Museum of Fine Arts, Boston. (Gift of Edward Jackson Holmes.) 29.1091.

97 Tea-pot, Paris, 1699/1700, by an unidentified master. Metropolitan Museum of Art, New York. (Bequest of Catherine D. Wentworth, 1948.) 48.187.78.

95

96

97

98   Tea-pot, Amsterdam, 1696, by Hendrik van Pruysen. Rijksmuseum, Amsterdam.

99   Tea-pot, Amsterdam, *c.* 1730, by Dirk van Hengel, master silversmith 1728-76 (?). Private collection.

100   Tea-pot, Copenhagen, 1760, by Christian Werum. Kunstindustrimuseet, Copenhagen. 33/1972.

made in a different receptacle from the one from which it was drunk.

During the first half of the seventeenth century the English began to imitate the Dutch sailors' habit of drinking tea. Snobbery was as important in upper-class English society in the seventeenth century as at any other time and this very expensive beverage was readily accepted. Here, too, the only receptacles that could be called—wrongly—'tea-pots' at that time are the kettle and the hot-water pot, but these are clearly distinguished from the tea-pot by the fact that they have no strainer at the base of the spout. From the seventeenth century onwards, china-ware became so fashionable that tea-drinkers used rice-alcohol pots for hot water. It was these pots on which silversmiths based the design of the first tea-pots.

No silver tea-pot is known to have existed in the Low Countries before the late seventeenth century. In England, on the other hand, the earliest pouring-vessel clearly intended to be used as a tea-pot, at least according to an inscription engraved on it, has been dated to 1670. At this time tea was still very dear, but was widely consumed in London. It was already being prepared in a different way. The

101   Tea-pot, Basle, *c.* 1725, by Hans Jacob Annony, master silversmith 1714-44. ▷ Private collection.

102 Design for a tea-pot, designed to qualify as a master, Basle, 1763, by Johann Ulrich IV Fechter, master silversmith 1764-96. Archiv der Hausgenossenzunft, Basle.

103 Tea-pot, work made to qualify as a master, Basle, 1764, by Johann Ulrich IV Fechter, master silversmith 1764-96. Private collection.

104 The silversmith John Singleton Copley, holding a tea-pot in his hand. Detail of portrait by Paul Revere (1735-1818), c. 1768-70. Museum of Fine Arts, Boston. (Gift of William B., Joseph W. and Edward H.R. Revere.) 30.781.

105 Tea-pot, Lausanne, c. 1765, by Elie Papus and Pierre-Henry Dautun, partners 1760-93. Private collection.

106 Tea-pot, Rome, *c.* 1725, by Angelo Spinazzi, master silversmith 1721-67. Kunstgewerbemuseum, Berlin (Staatliche Museen Preussischer Kulturbesitz). 97.169.

107 Design for a tea-pot, Italy, *c.* 1780, by an anonymous master. Cooper-Hewitt Museum, New York. 1938-88-4382.

squat, almost spherical form of tea-pot was based on Chinese pots used for pouring spirits. This shape, and the other features that distinguish the tea-pot from the coffee- or chocolate-pot, were largely retained in the centuries that followed.

In France tea did not become really well known as a medicinal drink until 1636. We have to wait until 1673 for the first reference, in a list, to a little vessel used for serving tea or clear soup, which may possibly be regarded as the prototype of the tea-pot.

Louis XIV seems never to have tried any of the colonial drinks, although he must have possessed several rare tea-pots, since there

are references in the inventory of his silverware to two tea-pots given by ambassadors from Siam in 1686; another is mentioned in 1701. Should we therefore conclude that these tea-pots were similar in shape to the pots then used for broth, known to us through the Stockholm drawings? Or would it be more correct to say that the same silver pots were used for both purposes? In France strainers did not appear at the base of the spout until quite late, during the first half of the eighteenth century. Does this indicate that hot water was still being poured on to tea in the same vessel as that from which it was drunk, and that the tea-pot was still really a kettle?

The earliest example of a Paris tea-pot that is still in existence is dated no earlier than 1720. There are older ones in Flanders, which is closer to Holland, especially in the port cities. Silver tea-pots have also been found in Marseilles and Bordeaux, but only later in the eighteenth century did they appear in French provincial towns. The first French tea-pots were usually pear-shaped, and therefore similar to those commonly encountered in England at the beginning of the eighteenth century. The long curved spout of these pots often has an animal's head at the tip. Silversmiths continued to decorated spouts in this way until the beginning of the nineteenth century. These animal heads remained very popular during the Empire period, not only in France but also in Germany and Switzerland.

Only two types of tea-pot were made in England during the early part of the eighteenth century. The first is pear-shaped; the second follows a Chinese model and is spherical. Both have very little decoration, even engraved. The spherical tea-pot continued to be popular throughout the eighteenth century and has been found not

108 Tea-pot and strainer, Lausanne, *c.* 1830, by Marc and Charles Gély, known as the Gély brothers, 1813-46. Musée de la Cathédrale, Lausanne. 92.

only in England, but also in all countries which English silverware reached: Scotland, North America, Portugal, Denmark and Switzerland. German and Swedish craftsmen followed the early eighteenth-century French prototype, but disfigured it by adding their own local decoration. The German courts readily accepted the fashion of tea-drinking from France. The first tea-service, including all the accessories such as a sugar-bowl, a cream- or milk-jug, a tea-caddy and a tray, as well as matching tea- and coffee-pots, was produced in Augsburg, which had a long reputation for its sets of silverware. These sets soon found their way to almost every part of Europe.

A pear-shaped type of tea-pot was almost simultaneously evolved in Holland. This type of vessel is characterized by excessive decoration.

109 *A Cup of Tea, c.* 1880. The tea-service on its tray must be the work of a silversmith resident in Philadelphia in the mid-19th century. Picture by Mary Cassatt (1844-1926). Museum of Fine Arts, Boston. (Mary Hopkins Fund.) 42.178.

110 Tea-service with tea-pot, milk-jug and sugar-bowl, Oporto, Portugal, 1836/43, by Joaquim Ferreira Godinho, master silversmith from 1805. Private collection.

The people of southern Europe were very reluctant to include tea-drinking among their gastronomic habits and continued faithfully to drink nothing but coffee. Silver tea-pots were unknown in Italy or Spain in the eighteenth century.

Tea was imported in great quantities into England at the end of Queen Anne's reign, with the result that its price fell and it became much more popular as a drink. By 1740 it had replaced coffee as the most fashionable drink and tea-pots were appearing in considerable numbers. In addition to the traditional types, English craftsmen were producing tea-pots in new shapes and with new kinds of decoration. Tea-pots, often richly adorned with rocaille work, which was fashionable in the mid-eighteenth century, were made at that time in the shape of caskets or inverted pears.

While this was happening in England, the silversmiths of Paris were exporting more tea-pots to other countries than they were making for the French market. Like the Germans, the French clearly preferred china tea-pots. Many German tea-sets have several silver-gilt articles but a china tea-pot. Silver tea-pots continued to be used only in the French ports.

Tea was brought into Russia by land from China and by 1740 it had already become a relatively cheap drink that was consumed at all levels of Russian society. It hardly needs to be said, however, that only the richest private individuals and families possessed silver or silver-gilt samovars. These great urns full of water with a built-in heating device are surmounted by little tea-pots, in which a very strong infusion of tea is kept warm.

In the neo-classical period English silversmiths returned to making tea-pots that were simpler in form, but extremely elegant. These were based either on ancient or on exotic models. One type which originated during that period, and is still popular today both in England and abroad, has an oval cylindrical body and a straight spout. Later, at the beginning of the nineteenth century, the luxury-loving English and French monarchs had these neo-classical shapes covered with rich ornamentation.

Tea-pots with ball feet were fashionable in Holland at the end of the eighteenth century, while pear-shaped tea-pots with little matching trays were popular in Norway and Denmark. Swedish silversmiths at this time produced a very large tea-pot with two spouts opposite each other, a feature that has never been satisfactorily explained. Swiss craftsmen adopted English prototypes, but were above all inspired by marvellous Flemish and Wallonian examples and succeeded in creating a very simple, elegant style of their own.

The Anglomania that prevailed at the end of the eighteenth century and throughout most of the nineteenth resulted in tea-drinking and its ceremonial trappings becoming popular even in those countries that had hitherto resisted tea. The Portuguese and even the Italians adopted the habit and their silversmiths created tea-pots based on English models. More and more complete tea services were produced—and not only in Augsburg or Russia, whose craftsmen had until then been the only ones to make them. Countless gadgets were also invented, during the nineteenth century especially: sugar-tongs, strainers, spoons for measuring tea, finger-bowls and so on. These served to complete the tea-set, which was a feature of almost every middle-class home at that time.

The Kettle and the Urn

In the preceding section we learned that the first tea-pots were really kettles with a lamp to keep the water inside them simmering until it was poured on to tea-leaves placed in a little china cup or tea-pot. Kettles have usually been made in quite large sizes, of copper or brass rather than of precious metal. A Paris inventory of

111　Kettle with two spouts, Göteborg, 1768, by Johan Christoffer Jungmarcker. Röhsska Konstslöjdmuseet, Göteborg.

100

112 Design for a hot-water urn with lamp, surmounted by a tea-pot, Germany, *c.*
1760. Musée des Arts Décoratifs, Paris. CD 4284, fol. 134.

113 Hot-water vessel with lamp, London, 1775/6, by a master silversmith with
the initials AF. Private collection.

114 The wife and children of John, 14th Lord Willoughby de Broke, taking tea. A large hot-water urn and, on a silver tray, a china tea-set can be seen. Detail of painting by Johann Zoffany (1733-1810). Private collection, England.

115 Hot-water urn with lamp, Copenhagen, 1808, by Abraham Nyemann. Kunstindustrimuseet, Copenhagen. 79/1952.

116 Design for an apparatus for boiling water, Augsburg, *c.* 1810, by J.A. Seethaler, master silversmith 1796-1835. Cooper-Hewitt Museum, New York. 1911-28-325.

115   116

1686, however, lists a silver kettle which is clearly a large pouring-vessel with a long curved spout, a swing handle at the top, a flat base and a lamp for burning embers or spirit. Very few of these silver tea-kettles have survived, but they can be seen in several eighteenth-century pictures of fashionable teas. Kettles of very high quality were made by the best silversmiths of the day. One really original masterpiece of international silverware was created at that time by Germain, the Paris craftsman. It is a kettle in the form of a low pagoda.

During the neo-classical period the kettle was often combined with the spirit-lamp to form a single monumental piece of silverware. About 1770 urns based on classical models were very popular, not only in England but also in Denmark, Portugal, Germany and Italy. These tea-urns were late to appear in France, but they became popular during the Empire period. Their design owed more to the Russian samovar than to any English model.

The *coquemar* and the *marabout* are very small kettles with a flat base and individual lamps which appeared in France in the mid-eighteenth century. Nowadays these little kettles and their lamps are often found separately.

The Chocolate-Pot

Chocolate was imported from Mexico into Spain from the sixteenth century onwards, but did not cross the Pyrenees until the mid-seventeenth century. Prepared in Spain from crushed cocoa-beans, it was introduced into France by the two seventeenth-century Spanish queens, Anne of Austria and Maria Teresa of Spain. The Sun King's wife remained very attached to Spanish customs all her life and was extremely fond of chocolate, which she had prepared by her servant, the celebrated Molina. The French court adopted the practice of drinking chocolate, first simply in imitation of the queen and then for preference, and the habit was firmly established in Paris by about 1670. Chocolate had to be boiled for a long time and stirred constantly. The container therefore needed to be solid enough for the drink to stay hot. Silver was the obvious material to choose, even more so than in the case of tea or coffee. What is strange is that the Spaniards had not thought to use it before the French did.

The vessel was shaped to suit the preparation of the drink. It was tall and usually pear-shaped, with a pierced lid so that the handle of the stirring-rod or 'swizzle-stick', with which the mixture of boiling water or milk and pieces of chocolate paste was stirred, could pass

Un Caualier, Et vne Dame beuuant du Chocolat
Ce jeune Caualier, et cette belle Dame   Mais l'on voit dans leurs yeux vne si viue flame
Se regalent de Chocolat;   Qu'on croit qu'il leur faudroit vn mets plus délicat .

117 A couple drinking chocolate. A maid-servant can be seen stirring the drink with a swizzle-stick. Print by N. Bonnart, *c.* 1690. Cabinet des Estampes, Bibliothèque Nationale, Paris.

through into the pot itself. Chocolate-pots were usually made with a swivelling finial on top of the lid. So that the chocolate mixture could be heated and to make sure that the pot remained stable, it was usually mounted on three feet that were high enough for a little spirit-lamp to be slipped underneath the body of the pot itself.

The earliest surviving chocolate-pot made by an English silversmith is dated 1685. Another, made ten years later, is clearly based on a French prototype, showing the influence of the French Huguenot craftsmen who came to England when the Edict of

118 Chocolate-pot, England, early 18th century, by Gabriel Sleath. Museum of Fine Arts, Boston. (Gift of Mrs. Christopher Hurd.) 1974-553.

119 Chocolate-pot, England, 1705, by Robert Cooper. Metropolitan Museum of Art, New York. (Gift of Irwin Untermyer, 1968.) 68.141.86.

120   Chocolate-pot, England, 1697, by Benjamin Bradford. Metropolitan Museum of Art, New York. (Gift of Irwin Untermyer, 1968.) 68.141.84.

121　Chocolate-pot, Turin. Hallmarks illegible. Private collection.

122　Chocolate-pot, Paris, 1780/1, by Alexandre de Roussy, master silversmith from 1758 to after 1792. Private collection.

Nantes was revoked. Although it is much more fragile, china was more popular than silver in northern Europe generally as a material for chocolate-pots in the eighteenth century.

The Coffee-Pot

Coffee was first brought to Europe from Arabia via Egypt in the middle of the seventeenth century. It was initially consumed in the ports at the end of trade routes from the eastern Mediterranean. It appeared almost simultaneously in Venice, Marseilles, London and Amsterdam. Like tea and chocolate, it was first taken in small quantities as a medicinal drink, but it was not long before its taste was appreciated and it became a very popular refreshment. The vogue for drinking coffee spread much more quickly than that for tea-drinking and it soon appeared in the salons of Paris as the fashionable drink *par excellence*. Although it is difficult to find a single reference to it around 1660, it was being drunk everywhere six years later. According to Furetière, it was the custom to drink coffee three times a day. Eleven years after its first appearance in Paris, it had to a very great extent replaced tea in public favour. This preference for coffee continued in France throughout the centuries that followed.

Coffee made its first appearance in London in 1637 and was drunk with such enthusiasm there until the end of the seventeenth century that, as in Paris, tea was almost excluded. It was only when the price of tea fell at the beginning of the eighteenth century that the English ceased drinking coffee and turned again to tea, which soon became the national drink.

Coffee is similar to tea and chocolate in that, when it first appeared in Europe, no receptacle was specifically associated with it as a drink. As soon as it had become popular at all levels of society, and especially in the fashionable salons, there was a clear need for an elegant vessel in which it could be prepared and from which it could be poured. To begin with, it would seem that vessels used for serving broth, chocolate-pots, kettles and tea-pots were all used for coffee. For a long time it was prepared only in the Turkish way, that is, it was boiled in and served from the same vessel. This was sufficient reason for coffee-pots to be made of silver and fitted with feet so that a little spirit-lamp could be placed underneath. Whereas

123 Drawing of a coffee-pot or chocolate-pot belonging to Louis XIV, Paris, *c.* 1700, attributed to Nicolas de Launay (1647-1727). Nationalmuseum, Stockholm. THC 835.

124 Drawing of a coffee-pot or vessel for serving broth, Paris, *c.* 1700, attributed to Nicolas de Launay (1647-1727). Kunstbibliothek, Berlin (Staatliche Museen Preussischer Kulturbesitz). Hdz 76.

125 Coffee-pot, France, early 18th century. No hallmarks. Private collection. ▷

109

126 Coffee-pot, Rome, *c.* 1760, by Giuseppe Grazioli, master silversmith 1749-92. Private collection.

127 Miniature coffee-pot or silversmith's model, Augsburg, hallmark 1767/9, but *c.* 1735, by Salomon Dreyer, master silversmith 1734-60. Private collection.

128 Coffee-pot or milk-jug, Mantua, 1792, by an unidentified master with the ▷ initials CC. Swiss National Museum, Zurich. LM 7298 b.

111

with the tea-pot the base of the spout was set very low on the body, in the case of the coffee-pot it had to be as high as possible, so that the coffee-grounds could settle and would not be poured into the cups. We know from seventeenth-century inventories that tea- and coffee-pots could only be distinguished at that time by their different spouts. Very few seventeenth-century coffee-pots have survived. The earliest English examples have been dated to about 1680 and the earliest French coffee-pot known today to 1705. A French drawing of 1702, preserved in Stockholm, shows the commonest prototype used in the late seventeenth and early eighteenth centuries. This prototype can be traced back to a number of different pouring-vessels that were commonly used in the seventeenth century, including ewers, jugs, vessels to hold wine and various Turkish or other oriental models made of metal or porcelain and used to prepare this exotic drink.

In England a type of coffee-pot was developed, the main elements of which have hardly changed at all throughout its history. The body is almost tubular, but round, oval or polygonal in cross-section. Its long spout is either straight or curved and the cover usually domed. The wooden or ivory handle is placed either at a right angle to the spout or directly opposite it. This English type of silver coffee-pot is seldom heavily decorated and never heavily engraved. The most elaborate decoration is found as a reinforcement of the soldered joints. This applied ornamentation consists of cut-card work in the form of flames or foliage. This type was normal until about 1735, after which date English coffee-pots were increasingly influenced by French models. Pear-shaped pots standing on three feet became very common. This style became more pronounced about 1765. In the mid-eighteenth century English coffee-pots were richly adorned with rocaille motifs and later with more simple floral garlands. In the neo-classical period their shape was based on that of Greek vases and urns, a fashion which persisted well into the nineteenth century and spread to other European countries.

The decoration of French coffee-pots evolved in much the same way, beginning with very sober and restrained ornamentation, becoming more contorted when rocaille work was favoured, and

129 Scene in a Venetian café. A coffee-pot is being presented on a silver salver by a servant and another servant is bringing a tray of cups. Fresco by Michelangelo Morlaiter, *c.* 1780. Palazzo Grassi, Venice.

130 Interior, showing a coffee-pot with three feet on the mantelpiece and a ▷ tea-pot on the *étagère*. Detail of picture by François Boucher, 1739. Musée du Louvre, Paris.

then more austere and elegant in the latter half of the eighteenth century. The fundamental features of the French coffee-pot, which persisted throughout the eighteenth century, were a pear-shaped body mounted on three feet, a flattened lid, a short spout rising from the base of the neck of the vessel and a wooden handle, sometimes straight and placed on the opposite side from the spout and sometimes set a right angle to the spout. The feet became longer and longer with the passage of time.

This basic model evolved by the silversmiths of Paris was so successful that it was followed not only in provincial France but also in the whole of Europe, with endless variations according to the individual town or district. Aix-en-Provence, Toulouse, Lyons, Bordeaux, Liège, Mons, Strasbourg, Basle, Berne and Geneva formed a wide circle around Paris where skilful craftsmen made coffee-pots that were very close to the Paris prototype, but differed from it in details of shape and decoration. It would be impossible to list all these details here, but it can be said that each place of production can be distinguished by the particular curve of the feet of its coffee-pots.

The choice of forms and decorative themes by German craftsmen has usually varied according to the prevailing taste in each centre of the country's silver industry, but in the case of coffee-pots a model was adopted that was based on the French prototype and brought to perfection by the silversmiths of Augsburg. Even though there was little sign in the eighteenth century of the inventive genius and high-quality workmanship which earned them such a reputation in the sixteenth and seventeenth centuries, their coffee-pots were very popular. They produced an enormous amount, competing with the makers of china-ware, and specialized in very rich decoration always in tune with the most recent fashion. They also continued to make complete sets of luncheon silverware, which always included one or two coffee-pots. Towards the middle of the eighteenth century Dresden, the capital of a great Polish and Saxon empire, became an important centre for silver; coffee-pots were made there in the shapes and with the decorative themes of Meissen china-ware.

In addition to models based on French and English prototypes, an original form known as the Turk's head was developed with

131 Coffee-pot, London, 1747/8, by William Cripps, master silversmith 1743-53. Private collection.

132 The Remy family in Bendorf, 1776. An open sugar container and a milk-jug ▷ can be seen on the table. The mother is pouring coffee from a coffee-pot that forms part of the set. Detail of group portrait by Januarius Zick. Germanisches Nationalmuseum, Nuremberg. GM 1380.

133 Coffee-pot, Paris, 1757, by François Thomas Germain, master silversmith 1748-91. Metropolitan Museum of Art, New York. (Joseph Pulitzer Bequest, 1933.) 33.165.1.

134 Coffee-pot, Stockholm, 1760, by Jakob Danielsson. Nordiska Museet, Stockholm.

135 Design for a coffee-pot, Stockholm, 1764, by Michael Åström. National-museum, Stockholm. NMH 180/1890.

136 Man-servant carrying a coffee-urn with a tap and a tray with cups; various tea- and coffee-pots in the rocaille-work frame. Anonymous print, Germany, mid-18th century.

137 Coffee-pot, Nuremberg, probably 1769/73, by G.N. Bierfreund, master silversmith 1740-84. Private collection.

138 Coffee-pot, Göteborg, 1744, by Johan Fredrik Pöpping. Röhsska Konstslöjdmuseet, Göteborg.

139

140

great success in northern Europe. It was not until relatively late that the coffee-pot with three feet was adopted in Denmark and Norway, where the squat type, similar to the tea-pot, was popular for a long time. All these vessels have a finial in the form of a bird in flight, which is highly characteristic of eighteenth-century Scandinavia. About 1760, however, there was an interest in neo-classical decoration rather than forms. This resulted in the production of some extremely curious and very original coffee-pots by Danish and Norwegian silversmiths.

Although French influence was very strong in Sweden throughout the eighteenth century, coffee-pots were made there in shapes and with ornaments that were directly dependent on Augsburg. The feet of these Swedish coffee-pots are decorated with foliage, their bodies and covers are adorned with garlands of flowers and fleurons, and there is rocaille work on their spouts.

The lasting popularity of coffee in Italy is clearly reflected in the impressive size of Italian coffee-pots. There are, however, individual differences in shape and decoration according to the region or town where they originated. Venetian silversmiths, with their traditional taste for oriental styles, produced coffee-pots in extremely contorted forms, with big bellies, high necks, turban-shaped covers and short spouts. The other great Italian centres of coffee-pots were Turin, Genoa, Rome, Bologna, Parma and Mantua. Turin pots were traditionally made in the French style, whereas those from Genoa were closer to the English model before it was influenced by France. The typical Genoese coffee-pot has a simple base without feet, a markedly domed lid and a long, curved spout. The Romans were extremely cosmopolitan in the eighteenth century and this led to a great variety of form and ornamentation in the coffee-pots produced in that city. They were usually very large and had a plain body which contrasted sharply with magnificently chased and decorated feet, lids and spouts. The silversmiths of

139 Coffee-pot known as a *marabout*, Paris, 1757/8, by Charles Donze, master silversmith 1756-77. Victoria and Albert Museum, London.

140 Coffee-pot or wine-pot, Oporto, *c.* 1770, by Luis Antonio Coelho. Fondação Ricardo Espirito Santo Silva, Lisbon.

141 Coffee-pot or pot used for serving broth, Geneva, mid-18th century, by an unknown master with the initials RIX. The coat of arms engraved on this pot is that of the Sellon family. Private collection.

142 Coffee-pot, Neuchâtel, *c.* 1760, by Samuel Bonvespre, mentioned before 1776. Private collection.

143 Coffee-pot, Lausanne, *c.* 1780, by Elie Papus and Pierre-Henry Dautun, partners 1760-93. Private collection.

141

142

143

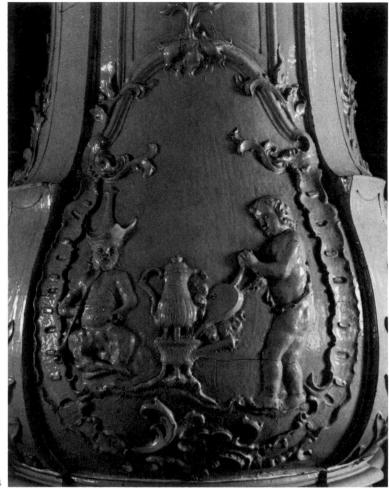

145

144 Cartouche on ceramic stove with two figures of angels, one heating coffee and the other smoking a pipe. Schloss Althausen, Germany.

145 Design for a coffee-pot in oriental style, Italy, *c.* 1740. Cooper-Hewitt Museum, New York. 1938-88-8128.

146 A Negro serving coffee. Fresco by Costantino Cedini (1741-1811), Padua, *c.* 1790. Library of the Palazzo Maldura, Padua.

147 Coffee-pot, Genoa, *c.* 1770, by an unknown master. Private collection.

148 Coffee-pot, Turin, *c.* 1780, by Giuseppe Vernoni. Museo Civico, Turin.

149

150

151

149 Silver-gilt coffee-pot, Strasbourg, 1789/90 according to the hallmarks, but made *c.* 1770 by Jean-Henry Oertel, master in 1749. Private collection.

150 Drawing of a neo-classical coffee-pot, Malmö, 1787, by Christian Silow. Museum, Malmö.

151 Design for a coffee-pot or wine-pot in antique style, Italy, *c.* 1790, attributed to Giovacchino Belli, master silversmith, 1787-1822. Cooper-Hewitt Museum, New York. 1938-88-5909.

152

153

152 Coffee-pot with lamp and stand, Hamburg, *c.* 1800, by Christian Arnold Hartrott, master 1798 – after 1807 (?). Private collection.

153 Coffee-pot, Philadelphia, *c.* 1790/1800, by Christian Wiltberger (1766-1851). Museum of Fine Arts, Boston. (Gift of Mr. John R. Farovid.) 61.949-53.

154-155 Coffee-pot with filter, Berne, *c.* 1835, by Georg Adam Rehfuss, active 1807-58. Private collection.

154

155

Bologna, Parma and Mantua were, like their fellow-craftsmen in Turin, strongly influenced by French coffee-pot design. French influence was also very strong in Spain, whereas Portuguese silversmiths followed the English more and more exclusively.

Coffee was enthusiastically accepted as a drink at a very early period in the Low Countries, where a very special form of coffee-pot was evolved, which was adopted only here and there in Flanders, Scotland and the Rhine valley. This Dutch vessel was really a great baluster- or pear-shaped fountain or cistern containing a mixture of coffee and milk, which was kept boiling all day. It was often placed in the middle of a table or on a smaller pedestal table and was usually equipped with three taps so that coffee could be taken from it. It has so far proved impossible to date this special type of coffee-pot precisely, but several examples still in existence today were undoubtedly made in Amsterdam at the turn of the seventeenth and eighteenth centuries.

From 1765-70 onwards, coffee-pots began to change their shape under the influence of neo-classicism, but it was not until the Directoire of 1795-9 that the traditional French coffee-pot was definitively abandoned in favour of an ovoid vessel more in accordance with the taste of the period. Under the Empire, the silversmiths of Paris produced work of such high quality that it became extremely popular everywhere in Europe. Throughout the nineteenth century the English and French types of coffee-pot existed side by side. In North America many different kinds of vessel were produced, according to whether the craftsmen making them were originally Dutch, Irish, English or German.

Flat Table-Ware

Plates

Although plates are nowadays almost always made of china or some form of crockery, this did not become general until the end of the seventeenth century. Silver plates are not much older and were found only in the homes of the wealthy. In 1538 King Francis I of France, who was a devotee of Italian art, ordered half a dozen round silver plates to be made, based on an Italian prototype. Even

156 Plate, North America (Massachusetts), c. 1690-1700, by Jeremiah Dummer (1645-1718). Museum of Fine Arts, Boston. (Spalding Collection.) 42.225.

157 Plate with wide rim, Lisbon, early 18th century. Hallmark of an unknown master. Private collection.

these were probably displayed on a silver buffet rather than used regularly at table. Equally ostentatious silver plates, engraved with historical themes, were also made at this time in sets of six at Antwerp and Nuremberg. These too were undoubtedly confined to the silver sideboards that added a touch of magnificence to the halls in which meals were taken.

During the sixteenth century plates as such were not generally used. Their place was taken by little round, square or oblong platters or trenchers. These utensils were usually of wood, but at more sumptuous tables they were sometimes made of pewter or even of silver. The wide-rimmed plate made of precious metal first appeared in Italy in the sixteenth century and north of the Alps at the beginning of the seventeenth century. These became more and more common on people's tables as eating habits changed. It was about this time that meat gradually ceased to be the almost exclusive basis of every meal and a more varied diet was adopted.

158   Plate with a wavy rim, bearing arms of the Hohenzollern-Hechingen family, Strasbourg, *c.* 1776, by F.D. Imlin (1757-1827). Private collection.

159   Two plates with arms of Frederick Augustus of Saxony, Dresden, 1772, by Carl David Schrödel, master silversmith from 1743. Private collection.

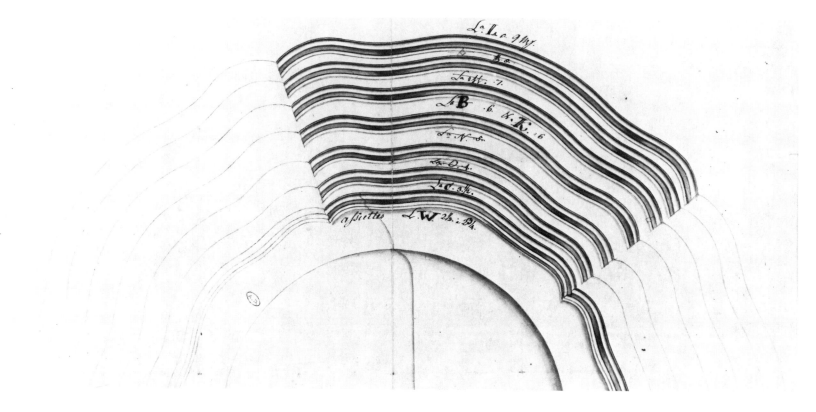

160 Design for a set of dishes and plates of different sizes, Germany, mid-18th century. Musée des Arts Décoratifs, Paris. CD 4284, fol. 75.

161 Design for a plate with a moulded rim and egg-shaped decorations, France, mid-18th century. Musée des Arts Décoratifs, Paris. CD 4284, fol. 63.

Louis XIV was particularly fond of silver and possessed a great number of gold, silver-gilt and silver plates. He ordered an especially fine set of table silver for his luxurious residence at Marly. The plates belonging to this service were remarkable for their narrow rims decorated with a delicately convoluted moulding. The term *marli*, which is now generally used in French for an 'inner rim' or 'inside edge', was originally applied to the moulded inner rims of this set of plates made for Louis XIV's palace of the same name. In the eighteenth century most plates had inner rims that were wrought and decorated like those of dishes. They were, however, never so excessively worked as they often were in the nineteenth century. Many silver plates were melted down from the late seventeenth century onwards because silver table-ware was coming to be replaced by china and porcelain plates imported from China or made in Europe.

Dishes

Like cups and beakers, dishes made of precious metal go back to the earliest times. Few examples of the large medieval silver dishes have survived, and those which do exist have deteriorated with long use. There are several wonderful Roman and Byzantine silver dishes, however, which vividly recall the splendid way in which meals were served at those times. In all periods a clear distinction has been made between dishes for common use and those for display. The

162 Still-life with dishes: a sauce-boat and a tureen and its salver, the latter based on a piece of silverware by Thomas Germain (1673-1748). Picture by François Desportes (1661-1743), Paris, 1726/8. Nationalmuseum, Stockholm, NM 800.

latter have, of course, always been the most beautiful, but unfortunately also the most readily dispensable pieces, and so have often landed in the melting-pot.

Despite so much destruction there are sufficient illustrations of dishes made as showpieces for us to have quite a good idea of their

163 Covered saucepan, Paris, 1787/8, by J.F.N. Caron. Metropolitan Museum of Art, New York. (Bequest of Catherine D. Wentworth, 1948.) 48.187.188 a, b.

164 Design for a dish of which the rim is decorated with egg-shaped ornamentation, France, mid-18th century. Musée des Arts Décoratifs, Paris. CD 4284, fol. 62.

165 Two dishes forming part of a set, London, 1745, by George Wickes. Private ▷ collection.

166 Large dish with draining-plate, London, 1745, by George Wickes. Private ▷ collection.

128

appearance. These masterpieces have very little in common with dishes that were intended for use at table. In the seventeenth century, these were still usually round, fairly deep and with a minimum of decoration, normally just the owner's arms engraved in the centre or on the rim.

In the eighteenth century the inner rims of dishes were decorated in as many ways as those of plates. They could be plain and flat, undulating, convoluted or moulded. Dishes were also made in very large sizes and in a great variety of shapes, according to the use to which they were to be put. Very often they were produced in sets, in which each dish was identical in form but of a different size.

Some examples of eighteenth-century dishes may be mentioned here: square vegetable dishes with rounded corners; concave dishes clearly intended for liquids; deep bowls, sometimes rectangular and sometimes round or oval, decorated with convoluted or festooned

167 Pair of vegetable dishes, Paris, 1775/6, by Jean Charles Duchesne, master silversmith from 1767 to after 1793. Private collection.

surfaces; large dishes with handles at the sides; oblong vessels to contain fish; and dishes with pierced base-plates for straining. Particular forms were also evolved for the special kinds of food favoured in each country or region. Very large, heavy round dishes with 'hemmed' rims, giving a very sumptuous impression, were made in Spain at this time. Throughout the eighteenth century the French form of service at table was current. This involved an arrangement of sets of twelve, eighteen or twenty-four identical dishes, sometimes placed on lamps, sometimes with lids, or else exhibited on dressers ready for serving and forming a magnificent background to the meal.

Dish-Covers

The way in which meals were served from the seventeenth century until the beginning of the nineteenth meant that it was always difficult to keep the food warm in dishes that were placed on the table before the commencement of the meal. The kitchens were generally a long way from the dining-room and it was therefore necessary to reheat the courses in a nearby pantry. Throughout the Middle Ages, and even as late as the eighteenth century, it was common to cover a dish containing food with another identical but inverted dish used as a lid; the two dishes were kept in position by a folded napkin. Often several dishes were carried one on top of another, and here again a folded serviette was used to hold them together. The dish or dishes would be taken to the dresser and the lid or lids removed before serving.

168   Design for a dish-cover with three different finials, France, c. 1750. Musée des Arts Décoratifs, Paris. CD 4284, fol. 98.

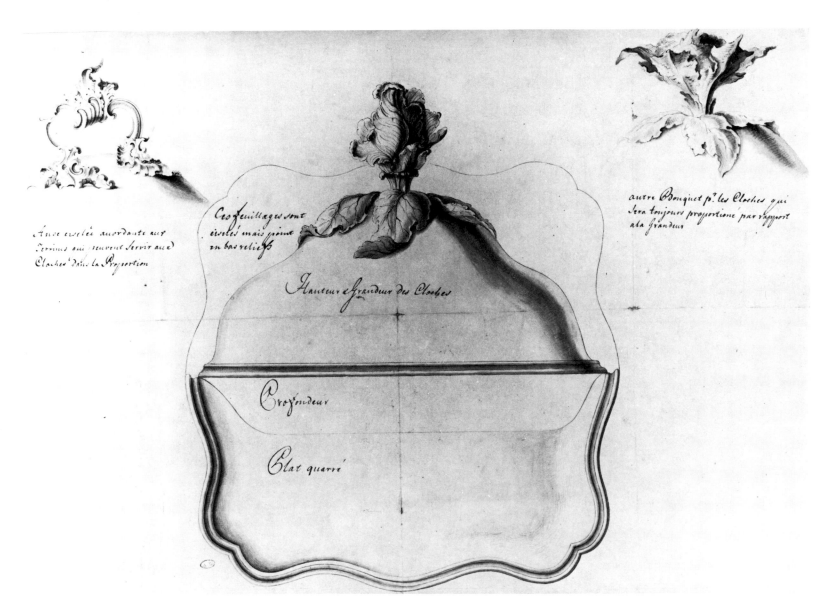

131

169 Square dish with cover decorated with foliage, Paris, 1756/60, by François Thomas Germain, master silversmith 1748-91. Museu Nacional de Arte Antiga, Lisbon.

170 Design for a rocaille dish-cover richly adorned with vegetable and floral motifs, Augsburg, *c.* 1750. Musée des Arts Décoratifs, Paris. CD 4284, fol. 99.

171 Dish-cover, Paris, 1772/3, by Jacques Nicolas Roëttiers. Rijksmuseum, Amsterdam. RBK 17023.

In the French mode of service the table was set with dishes containing food before the diners arrived. The dish-cover was invented to keep the contents warm. It was not long before its decorative effect became as important as its function. Round dishes had hemispherical covers and vegetable dishes had lids with four panels. On top there was always a knop or finial, which could in some cases be folded back.

These dish-covers were often real masterpieces and were made by the best silversmiths of the period. They were, of course, seen only on the tables of the wealthiest people. When the French form of service died out in the early nineteenth century, this virtually marked the end of the dish-cover, few of which survive today.

Trays, Salvers and Coasters

Silver trays hardly existed before the nineteenth century, but very many were produced at that time to accompany tea- and coffee-sets, especially under the Empire. They were the counterpart in silver of the china or porcelain breakfast-trays that abounded in the eighteenth century. They can be traced back to the very large serving dishes with two handles, one at each end.

From the sixteenth century to the nineteenth salvers were made in profusion. These were small circular trays standing on a central foot or stem, frequently used at table to serve glasses or in the toilet-service to present scented gloves. They are often mentioned in inventories, where they are variously called salvers, waiters or

172   Design for a salver, Paris, *c.* 1700. From the Tessin Collection. National-museum, Stockholm. THC 849.

173   Salver, Augsburg, 1737/9, by Johann Heinrich Darjes, master silversmith 1733-60. Private collection.

coasters. Food might be offered ceremonially on a tray or salver to avoid it having to be cut by a servant. At a time when wine was never drunk neat but always diluted with water, glasses were served on a salver along with a pair of decanters, one for wine and the other for water.

The salver originated in Italy and continued to be widely used there. It was adopted in France and Germany during the seven-

174   Design for a salver with detail of the foot and rim, Augsburg, *c.* 1750. Musée des Arts Décoratifs, Paris. CD 4284, fol. 69.

175   Little serving tray with a porcelain *trembleuse*, an engraved glass and a little ▷ raised saucer for delicacies, Augsburg, 1755/7, by Johann Jacob Adam. Kunstgewerbemuseum, Berlin (Staatliche Museen Preussischer Kulturbesitz). 96.209.

176 Silver-gilt salver, Paris, *c.* 1805, by Martin Guillaume Biennais (1764-1843). Silberkammer der Residenz, Munich.

177 A man-servant holding a silver tray with sorbets and flagons of water. Detail of a fresco by Michelangelo Morlaiter (1729-1806). Palazzo Grassi, Venice.

178 Round tray engraved with chinoiseries, London, *c.* 1685, by an unidentified master with the initials S.H. Museum of Fine Arts, Boston. (Theodora Wilbour Fund.) 50.2724-5.

179 Design for a tray, the rim of which is decorated with hunting trophies, ▷ Germany, *c.* 1740. Musée des Arts Décoratifs, Paris. CD 4284, fol. 68.

136

180 Large silver tray, Austria, 1830, by a master with the initials HM. Unidentified hallmarks. Private collection.

teenth century. Salvers also appeared in England at that time, but the custom was then abandoned. The flat surface often had many foils and was usually engraved in the centre with the owner's coat of arms. In the nineteenth century this basically ceremonial piece of silverware lost its original function and also many of its earlier features, especially its pedestal, which had in any case never been very stable. In this way it developed into the small round tray that became so common.

Shaped Table-Ware

Tureens

These receptacles with bulging bellies for holding soup and similar foods on the table, usually known in English as tureens, have always been objects of great ostentation. They have been made in various sizes. The largest type of tureen, the *pot à oille*, can be traced back to the court of Louis XIV where, according to an explanation offered by Madame de Sévigné which cannot, unfortunately, be verified, it was invented to contain a Spanish dish. These very big tureens were apparently introduced into France by Maria Teresa of Austria, who was fond of an exquisite kind of hotpot consisting of tender meat, truffles, rare vegetables and a mixture of aromatic herbs. This choice dish deserved to be presented in a receptacle of equal excellence.

Another kind of tureen, the *soupière*, which differs from the 'Spanish' tureen only in size, first appeared in France in 1729. By the end of the century this diminutive vessel was widely used in that country. It appeared in England during the reign of Queen Anne. The earliest known example has been dated to 1723. A third form of tureen, the *terrine*, was used to hold soups and stews of various kinds. It is large and either rectangular in shape with panelled sides, or else oblong or oval.

181 Soup-tureen with its salver, engraved with arms of the dukes of Bavaria, ▷ Paris, 1705, by Claude II Ballin, master silversmith 1661-1754. Silberkammer der Residenz, Munich.

138

182 Soup-tureen, one of a pair belonging to the treasure of the kings of Saxony. Dresden, 1719/22, by Paul Ingermann, master silversmith 1698-1747. Private collection.

183 Design for a tureen, Rome, *c.* 1730. Cooper-Hewitt Museum, New York. 1938-88-6007.

184 Drawing of a soup-tureen, Rome, *c.* 1700. Cooper-Hewitt Museum, New York. 1938-88-8126.

185 Design for a tureen, Augsburg, *c.* 1750. Musée des Arts Décoratifs, Paris. CD 4284, fol. 91.

186 Design for a tureen decorated with hunting themes, Augsburg, *c.* 1760. Musée des Arts Décoratifs, Paris. CD 4284, fol. 122, Pl. 2.

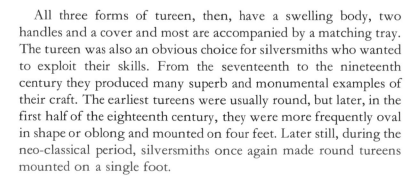

187 Design for a tureen with papal coat of arms, Rome, early 18th century. Cooper-Hewitt Museum, New York. 1938-88-5925.

All three forms of tureen, then, have a swelling body, two handles and a cover and most are accompanied by a matching tray. The tureen was also an obvious choice for silversmiths who wanted to exploit their skills. From the seventeenth to the nineteenth century they produced many superb and monumental examples of their craft. The earliest tureens were usually round, but later, in the first half of the eighteenth century, they were more frequently oval in shape or oblong and mounted on four feet. Later still, during the neo-classical period, silversmiths once again made round tureens mounted on a single foot.

In decorating tureens, silversmiths often let their imagination run riot. The rich and varied themes include fruit and vegetables, flowers and animals, classical ornamentation and rocaille work. It was the exuberant nature of this decoration that gave rise to the heated controversy between the ancients and the moderns that was unleashed when Charles-Nicolas Cochin published his famous *Supplication aux Orfèvres* in 1754.

188 Large oval tureen on its salver, Augsburg, *c.* 1725, by Jakob Waremberg, ▷ master silversmith 1711-58. Private collection.

142

189 Design for a soup-tureen, attributed to Thomas Germain, master silversmith 1673-1748, Paris, *c.* 1740. Cooper-Hewitt Museum, New York. 1911-28-160.

190 Tureen on its salver, London, 1740, by Paul Crespin ▷ (1694-1770). Museum of Art, Toledo, U.S.A. (Gift of Florence Scott Libbey, 1964.) 64.51.

144

146

◁ 191 Soup-tureen, London, 1820/1, by Paul Storr, master silversmith 1792-1834. Devonshire Collection, Chatsworth House, England.

192 Design for a large soup-tureen with different variants for the decoration on either side, by Johann Alois Seethaler, master silversmith 1796-1835. Cooper-Hewitt Museum, New York. 1911-28-360.

In every part of Europe the tureen has for centuries always held pride of place as the most important piece of silverware on the table. Its form and decoration have evolved with the passage of time, and it is easier to measure the evolution of taste from the tureen than from almost any other piece of shaped silver table-ware. We may also compare the products not only of different countries and regions, but even of different workshops and individual craftsmen. The most outstanding pieces have undoubtedly come from France and England, but Italian and German silversmiths have also made superb and beautifully finished tureens, as have master craftsmen in a number of other countries with an aristocratic culture.

147

148

193 Soup-tureen with its salver, Berne, *c.* 1825, by Georg Adam Rehfuss, master silversmith 1807-58. Private collection.

194 Design for a tureen with arms of the King of Sweden, standing on its salver, Paris, *c.* 1775. Kunstbibliothek, Berlin (Staatliche Museen Preussischer Kulturbesitz). Hdz 4137.

195 Covered bowl, Paris, 1672/3, by an unidentified master silversmith. Victoria and Albert Museum, London.

The Bowl or Porringer

By 'bowl' I mean a large covered vessel or cup with two lugs or flat thumbplates, one on either side; this was a very common piece of table silverware in the seventeenth and eighteenth centuries. It originated much earlier, of course, and its classical shape is derived from that of the wine-cup, wine-taster or brandy-cup. The bowl was, in a sense, a marginal item in the table service and was often used only to serve food to those who were confined to bed. Its German name is *Wöchnerinnenschüssel* or 'bowl for a woman in confinement'; which shows clearly enough that a silver bowl of this type would be given to a young mother as a present. These bowls were not used exclusively by women and, from the sixteenth century onwards, became customary for drinking clear meat soup or broth. Later, they were made in larger sizes and were then used only to contain boiled meat served in its own gravy.

Before the introduction of china-ware, bowls of this kind were almost always made of silver, which enabled the food in them to be kept warm. This also explains why some bowls are very simple, whereas others are mignificent. In the eighteenth century the bowl was frequently used as a little tureen and its lid, which originally had three or four feet shaped in various ways, often served as a little plate or cup for scraps left over from the meal. The plate or tray, which habitually accompanied the bowl in the eighteenth century,

196 Bowl or *écuelle*, Zurich, 1694, by Dietrich Meyer, master silversmith 1675-1733. Swiss National Museum, Zurich. LM 54111.

197 Design for a bowl with a lid which has four little feet so that it could be used as a plate, Germany, *c.* 1740. Musée des Arts Décoratifs, Paris.CD 4284, fol. 120, Pl. 2.

198 Bowl or *écuelle* without a lid, Paris, 1753/4, by Sébastien Igonet, master silversmith from 1725 to after 1766. Private collection.

199 Travelling-case with a bowl, plate, spice-box and knife, fork and spoons, Augsburg, 1710/12, by Paul Solanier, master silversmith 1666-1724. Private collection.

200 Silver-gilt covered bowl or *écuelle* on its salver-dish, Strasbourg, 1773/6, by ▷ Jacques Henry Alberti, master silversmith 1764-95. Private collection.

201 Porringer or caudle-cup, North America (Massachusetts), 1684, by Jeremiah Dummer (1645-1718). Museum of Fine Arts, Boston. (Lent by the Third Religious Society.) 821.10.

202 Cup with two handles, England, *c.* 1660, by an unknown master working in the style of P. van Vianen. Museum of Fine Arts, Boston. (Theodora Wilbour Fund.) 60.534.

goes back to a period when it was no longer used for its original purpose.

The silver bowl has been produced in almost every European country. One of the earliest examples is a silver-gilt bowl with lugs which belonged to the Emperor Charles V. It has been known in France since about 1620. At that time the only parts of the bowl that were adorned were the two lugs or flat handles. By the mid-seventeenth century it had become a common piece of silverware in France, where it was known as the *écuelle*, and served a variety of purposes.

Th *écuelle* as such has never been widely used in English-speaking countries, where another, but very similar silver article has taken its place. This is the porringer, which is basically a large, tall cup, often covered, with a handle on either side. Porringers were made in great abundance in England until well into the nineteenth century and gave English craftsmen an excellent opportunity to create silver objects as sumptuous as any produced abroad. These porringers were designed to be displayed on silver sideboards and buffets rather than to be used. It is therefore hardly surprising that trophies or 'cups' awarded for success in sport are still made in this basic form. Originally, the porringer was similar in shape to the classical urn with two handles and a cover. About 1660 it became almost cylindrical and looked more like a beer-tankard. This development was checked by the arrival of French silversmiths, who preferred a beaker-shaped porringer mounted on a little pedestal or base, at first of plain silver but later highly decorated. Around 1730 the porringer ceased to be used at all and became a mere showpiece. During the neo-classical period it was highly favoured, because its basic shape was so close to that of a Greek urn.

A relatively shallow bowl was often used in France and elsewhere as a bleeding-bowl or cup. Another type was the so-called 'quaich' made in Scotland until about 1730. This was a large bowl based on the great Baltic and Scandinavian vessels for brandy or spirits. Very luxurious bowls, based on French models, were also produced in Italy, especially in Piedmont. Most of them date from the eighteenth century.

The bowl was also very popular in Germany, where it formed an essential part of the set of utensils made for travelling. These sets were produced almost exclusively by the silversmiths of Augsburg throughout the eighteenth century. German bowls often have many flat surfaces and are richly chased or engraved. They also formed part of the toilet-sets so common at that time. As we have already

203 Two-handled porringer, England, *c.* 1640, attributed to the silversmith P. ▷ van Vianen. Museum of Fine Arts, Boston. (Theodora Wilbour Fund.) 63.1254.

153

seen, broth was drunk from such bowls at the lunch often served during the morning toilet preparations or when rising from bed. The present-day French practice of drinking coffee with milk at breakfast or chocolate from large bowls may be a survival of this earlier habit. When deep plates for soup and soup-tureens came to be used and eating habits changed at the end of the eighteenth century, however, bowls and porringers of the kind described here ceased to be made.

The Sauce-Boat

The practice of serving hot sauces separately from the meat or fish is a clear sign that cooking and the preparation and service of meals had reached a new level of refinement in the eighteenth century. The oval or boat-shaped sauce-container with a lip for pouring at

204　Pair of covered cups with two handles, London, *c.* 1680. Hallmarks of a master silversmith with the initials RC. Museum of Fine Arts, Boston. (Theodora Wilbour Fund.) 66.284-5.

205　Sauce-boat, England, *c.* 1740, probably by Nicholas Sprimont. Museum of ▷ Fine Arts, Boston. (Jessie and Sigmund Katz Fund.) 1973.529.

each end and a handle on either side goes back, like the bowl, to the brandy-cup. This form of sauce-boat was based on a prototype found in Louis XIV's inventories of silverware from 1700 onwards. It changed very little subsequently, apart from its lips. From 1720 onwards it can also be found in England, where it usually has a deeper body. The same can be said of sauce-boats

◁ 206 Pair of sauce-boats, Saint-Quentin, France, 1768/75, by Pierre-Adrien Dachery, master craftsman 1765-after 1781. Metropolitan Museum of Art, New York. (Bequest of Catherine D. Wentworth, 1948.) 48.187.13, 14.

◁ 207 Sauce-boat with saucer and ladle, England, *c.* 1750, by Nicholas Sprimont. Museum of Fine Arts, Boston. (Jessie and Sigmund Katz Fund.) 1971.776.

208 Sauce-boat, Stockholm, 1819, by Erik Adolf Zethelius, master silversmith 1803-39. Nordiska Museet, Stockholm.

209 Design for a sauce-boat, Augsburg, *c.* 1810, by J.A. Seethaler, master silversmith 1796-1835. Cooper-Hewitt Museum, New York. 1911-28-340.

made in Scandinavia. Throughout the eighteenth century the boat-shaped vessel was normally used for sauces in German-speaking countries, the only difference being that four little feet made in the form of volutes replaced the little central pedestal.

Was it purely by chance that these boat-shaped sauce-containers appeared at much the same time as the medieval nef was disappearing from the table? Whether this is so or not, it certainly seems that diners have liked to have an object made in the form of a boat on the table—either a German-style hanap or a sauce-boat in the English or French tradition.

A differently shaped sauce-boat appeared at almost exactly the same time as the one described above, that is, during the first decades of the eighteenth century. This type is still boat-shaped, but has only one lip and a handle at the opposite end. It is very close to the pouring-vessel, pot or jug, and also to the hanap designed in the form of a nef or a nautilus cup; sometimes it was shell-shaped. This kind of sauce-boat was extremely popular in England until the late nineteenth century. Rocaille work became fashionable throughout Europe in the eighteenth century and the sauce-boat clearly lent itself readily to this animated style, flowing with sinuous movement. French silversmiths even went so far as to imitate the

oyster-shells and the cartilaginous waves of seventeenth-century Flemish, Dutch and Italian masters of the decorative arts.

These two types of sauce-boat continued to be produced without any fundamental change in shape throughout the rest of the eighteenth and the nineteenth centuries. Silver sauce-boats became quite monumental and often served merely to decorate the banqueting-tables of the wealthy. Very few were produced in the Low Countries, Scandinavia or Switzerland. In Italy, where porcelain and china-ware remained popular for so long, they were not made of silver until the early nineteenth century.

The most serious disadvantage of the sauce-boat is that it has no lid. To overcome the problem of loss of heat, the traditional sauce-boat was replaced in England by a small version of the tureen. These covered sauce-tureens usually had a slot for the spoon or sauce-ladle. To avoid making the table-cloth dirty, a little tray or dish was often fixed to the foot of the sauce-boat from the end of the eighteenth century onwards. The ultimate peak of perfection in sauce-vessels was reached in 1780 or thereabouts, when the Duke of Argyle invented the gravy-server that is named after him. The argyle is heated internally by embers or boiling water, so that the sauce or gravy is kept warm.

210 Egg-cup, Augsburg, *c.* 1635/40, by Salomon II Rittel, master silversmith 1608-49. Private collection.

211 Egg-cup for an egg placed horizontally. The foot can be used to serve the egg upright. Augsburg, 1763/5, by Johann Jakob Adam, master silversmith 1748-91. Private collection.

212 Egg-cup, Paris, 1725/6, by Aymé Joubert, master silversmith 1703 — before 1747. Metropolitan Museum of Art, New York. (Bequest of Catherine D. Wentworth, 1948.) 48.187.285.

213 Egg-cup, Paris, 1764/5, by François Thomas Germain, master silversmith 1748-91. Museu Nacional de Arte Antiga, Lisbon.

The Egg-Cup

Eggs have for so long been eaten during meals that the objects designed to hold them have been as elegant and as luxurious as the rest of the tableware. The shape of the container has been determined by the way eggs are usually served in the country concerned.

There are only two practical ways of doing this. The earliest way, which for a long time was the most common, was to lay the egg down horizontally in a little oval boat. The earliest examples, found in the first half of the seventeenth century, are German. In the eighteenth century they were made above all in Augsburg and Strasbourg and were included in toilet-services. In the Low Countries, the German tradition of serving eggs lying down persisted for a long time.

The method employed in France and other Latin countries was different. There, eggs were served upright in an egg-cup of basically the type that is so familiar today. In the eighteenth century, however, egg-cups were produced in all possible variants of the baluster shape, many of them extremely picturesque. Louis XV was particularly fond of boiled eggs and had several elegant egg-cups made for himself in 1727, thus initiating a fashion for eating eggs in this way. According to the tradition followed at the Swedish court, at gala dinners there was always a gold egg-cup beside the royal place at table. This tradition probably originated in the ceremonial observed at Louis XV's little suppers.

Both ways of serving eggs were practised at the German courts, where the example of eighteenth-century France was followed. Several delightful pieces of silverware were made at Dresden in which both forms of service are combined in a single cup: the egg can either be laid down horizontally in the foot or placed upright in the cup itself.

In the nineteenth century more and more boiled eggs were eaten, with the result that many different kinds of egg-boilers and coddlers were invented and then made by silversmiths.

Salt-Cellars

Salt has always been extremely important. This indispensable condiment has at times been the object almost of a cult, and this attitude is reflected in the way it has traditionally been presented at table. The ceremonial surrounding its use in the Middle Ages survived until the nineteenth century. People of all classes have always respected salt and the use of silver salt-cellars has never been

214   Salt, England, end of 16th century. No hallmarks. Museum of Fine Arts, Boston. (Gift in Memory of Charlotte Beeche Wilbour.) 33/62.

215   Pair of salt-cellars, Biberach an der Riss, Germany, *c.* 1600, with illegible maker's marks. Swiss National Museum, Zurich. LM 10048 a, b.

216　Double salt surmounted by a caster, Valladolid, *c.* 1590, by José de Madrid. Victoria and Albert Museum, London. 180-1956.

217　Bell salt, surmounted by a caster, London, *c.* 1614, by an unidentified master with the initials HM. Museum of Fine Arts, Boston. (Bequest of Frank Brewer Bemis.) 35.1556.

restricted to royal households. From the Middle Ages until as late as the nineteenth century, kings and other important personages kept their salt in locked containers—nefs, cadenas and salts—because it can easily be confused with powdered arsenic and rulers have always feared being poisoned.

More silverware has been preserved in England than on the Continent. That country still treasures some medieval salts which are undoubtedly similar to those then in use elsewhere in Europe. A treatise on courtesy which appeared in 1475 contains a recommendation that salt should be served on the tip of a little knife and that food should not be dipped into the salt container. Despite this advice, however, the latter practice continued all over Europe until the seventeenth century.

To prevent the salt from being spread on the table, it was kept in lump form in the salt-cellar. One salt was usually placed at the right-hand side of the place set for the master of the house. This was sometimes of monumental dimensions. A smaller container was frequently set at the other end of the table. In the fourteenth century salts were often made in remarkable, even freakish shapes, but this practice was abandoned during the sixteenth century, when the vogue for the freakish was transferred to the hanap. Towards the end of the Middle Ages salts were often made in the form of an hour- or sand-glass. The bell salt, which was wider at the base than at the top, was also common. Some salts were cylindrical or square, while others consisted of two or more containers fitted one on top of the other. These very tall salts were produced above all in the

218 Salt surmounted by a caster, Lisbon, *c.* 1650, by an unidentified master with the initials IL. Fondação Ricardo Espirito Santo Silva, Lisbon.

219 Salt, North America, *c.* 1680, by Jeremiah Dummer (1645-1718). Museum of Fine Arts, Boston. (Bequest of Charles Hitchcock Tyler.) 32.371.

northern countries of Europe. In the south salts were usually shorter and less elaborate; frequently they were triangular, were mounted on little feet, and had a round cavity for the salt. Many very ornate vessels were melted down or sacrificed to changing fashion, although we can often gain an idea of their shape and decoration from surviving salt-cellars of porcelain. In the sixteenth century Spanish silversmiths made salts which were cylindrical, had two containers, placed one above the other, and were surmounted by a domed cover. A very similar type was produced at this time in Flanders.

In the seventeenth century a form based on the earlier hour-glass salt was produced almost everywhere in Europe. It first appeared in about 1630 and survived until the nineteenth century. It was cylindrical in shape, but wider at the top and bottom than in the middle. The decoration was engraved or chased according to local taste. In France and Italy this was the most classical form. It usually had many architectural features, such as an oval or circular bowl set on a fluted stem or column and a round or polygonal base. In

220 Salt, Amsterdam, 1646, by A. Griel. Stedelijk Museum, Amsterdam.

221 Pair of salts in English style, Lausanne, *c.* 1760, by Elie Papus and Pierre-Henry Dautun, partners 1760-93. Private collection.

222 Double salt- or spice-box, Paris, 1748/9, by Pierre-Aymé Joubert, master silversmith 1735-63. Metropolitan Museum of Art, New York. (Bequest of Catherine D. Wentworth, 1948.) 48.187.380.

223 Three salts with pierced lids. *Left and centre*: a pair, Berlin, *c.* 1770, by Henry Masseron, master silversmith 1767-1817. *Right*: a single salt, Breslau, *c.* 1770, by a master with the initials MA. Private collection.

224 Pair of covered salts, Paris, 1750/1, by Jean-François Balzac, master silversmith 1749-66. Private collection.

220

221

222

162

223

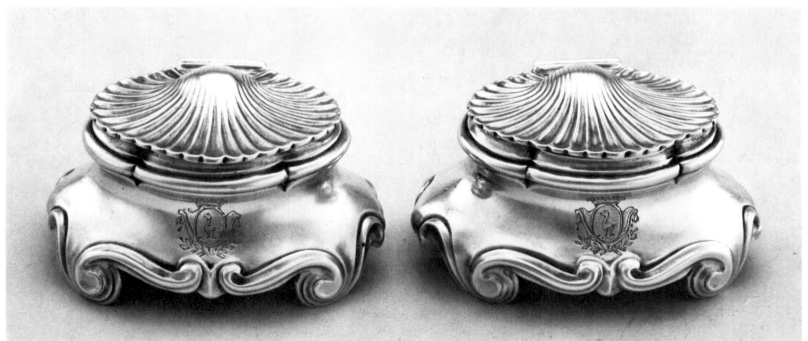

224

163

226 Design for a salt or pepper container, Rome, *c.* 1800, by Giovacchino Belli, master silversmith 1787-1822. Cooper-Hewitt Museum, New York. 1938-88-650.

northern Europe these characteristics of the hour-glass salt were obscured by the great profusion of ornamentation. Many of these salts had little feet on the upper rim, on which it was possible to place a lid.

New forms were invented during the second half of the eighteenth century. These salts were much smaller and were generally made in sets, so that each person at table could have one in front of him. From this time onwards salt-cellars were fundamentally little boxes with lids, often hinged; sometimes they had several compartments, each containing a different powdered spice. The most common condiments and spices at this time were salt, pepper and nutmeg. If the nutmeg was kept as a nut, there was usually a little grater in the middle of the box for the nut to be grated as and when required. Little tubular graters were placed between the two hinged lids of double-lidded spice-boxes, which were produced mainly in England and France.

A box with two compartments and a single lid, rather like a snuff-box in appearance, was invented by Augsburg silversmiths in the early eighteenth century. It was usually of silver-gilt and became as fashionable as a snuff-box. There was always a spice-box of this kind in all the great sets of table utensils for the individual diner, and it was in constant use throughout the meal.

When rocaille work was fashionable, salts were often made by English and French silversmiths in shell form. Later, the taste for neo-classical design made craftsmen more restrained and salt was served in little glass or cut-glass containers, either transparent or coloured blue, in silver mountings with pierced galleries. Keeping the salt in glass prevented the silver or silver-gilt from being corroded. This practice was quickly adopted throughout Europe. The age of the monumental salt had by this time passed and the small individual salt-cellar had become universally accepted.

Pepper-Pots

The practice of flavouring food that was otherwise monotonous with condiments and spices was commoner in the north of Europe than in the south, at least until the eighteenth century. Until then pepper was imported into Europe only by Portuguese merchants, who jealously preserved their monopoly. Because it was such an expensive commodity, it was kept in boxes and only small quantities were ground before being served at table. The table pepper-mill is a modern invention and has no early counterpart.

◁ 225 Pair of double salt-cellars, Paris, 1779/80, by Marc-Etienne Janety, master silversmith 1777-93. Private collection.

227 Pair of pepper-pots, Zurich, *c.* 1640, by Hans Heinrich Kitt, master silversmith 1625-65. Swiss National Museum, Zurich. LM 10049 a, b.

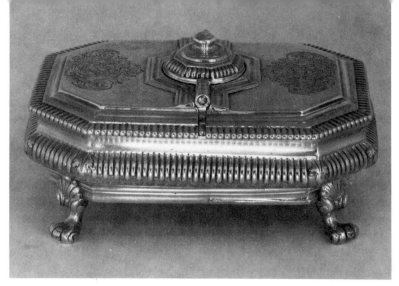

228 Double salt- or spice-box with a nutmeg-grater in the middle, Paris, 1723/4, by Nicolas Mahon, master silversmith 1719-33. Metropolitan Museum of Art, New York. (Bequest of Catherine D. Wentworth, 1948.) 48.187.273 a, b.

229 Double salt-cellar with lid, Lausanne, *c.* 1750, by Pierre Masmejan, mentioned from 1752 onwards, and Elie Papus, master silversmith, 1752-93.

230 Little spice-caster, Burgdorf, Switzerland, *c.* 1750, by an unidentified master with the initials HAK. Private collection.

231 Little pepper- or cinnamon-caster with arms of Neuchâtel, probably Berne, *c.* 1780. No hallmarks. Private collection.

Little powder-flasks much like those used for gunpowder have, however, been found among silver table-ware from the sixteenth century onwards. A little later miniature casters were made, which could be filled either with pepper or with some other powdered spice. To preserve the aroma of the contents, the pierced lids of these pepper-casters could be closed by turning them so that an unpierced lining slid underneath. From the seventeenth century onwards, receptacles with two compartments were often made for pepper and salt. This type was produced more and more frequently during the second half of the eighteenth century, when salt-cellars were provided with matching pepper-bowls.

Sugar Containers

Sugar was a rare commodity until the end of the sixteenth century. It continued to be expensive until long after that time and was therefore not only used very sparingly but also surrounded by a certain amount of ceremony. It was taken in two distinct forms: as lumps and as powder. Among the different receptacles and utensils for serving it at table are the sugar-box, sugar-caster, perforated sugar-spoon and, later, sugar-tongs.

We are very badly informed about the shape of sugar containers in seventeenth-century France, where most of these objects were invented. No sugar containers from that period have survived and little precise information about them is given in inventories compiled before the eighteenth century. Cardinal Mazarin may have introduced them into France and his inventory is the only one to list sugar-boxes together with their spoons. It does not, however, provide any details about the shape of these boxes. The reference is none the less valuable in that it proves that sugar was at that time

232 Sugar-caster, Paris 1709/19, by André David, master silversmith 1703-43 (?). Metropolitan Museum of Art, New York. (Bequest of Catherine D. Wentworth, 1948.) 48.187.73 a.

233 Sugar-caster from Louis XIV's collection. Drawing by Nicolas de Launay (1647-1727). Nationalmuseum, Stockholm. THC 834.

234 Two designs for sugar-casters, Italy, c. 1710. Cooper-Hewitt Museum, New York. 1938-88-8127.

168

served in powder form. This practice continued until the end of the eighteenth century. Richelet's *Dictionary*, which appeared at the end of the seventeenth century, and the famous *Encyclopaedia* of Diderot and d'Alembert in the middle of the following century both mention sugar containers *(sucriers)*; the modern French term *saupoudroir* then referred to a utensil for sprinkling powder on wigs.

The sugar-caster was invented in France and was always quite large, although miniature versions were used for spices. In its earliest form it was basically a cylinder with a pierced domed lid surmounted by a knop or finial, fastened to the body by a bayonet socket. Several English sugar-casters made in the mid-seventeenth century and some French casters dating back to the end of that century are examples of this original design. About the turn of the seventeenth to the eighteenth century the sugar-caster became less ponderous and more elegant. These baluster-shaped casters were made almost everywhere. The finest examples come from Paris, but very handsome ones were also produced in Bordeaux and Marseilles, both ports where ships unloaded their cargoes of sugar from the Antilles.

The sugar-caster was soon accepted throughout Europe. It appeared almost simultaneously in France, Italy and England. By the middle of the eighteenth century, it had also appeared in the Low Countries and Scandinavia, but by this time it had ceased to be fashionable in France. Sugar had by then become so widely used that sugar-bowls or containers in the form of little tureens were preferred.

One of the most striking and original creations of French silversmiths were silver sugar-bowls imitating bowls of fruit, of the kind usually made of porcelain or china. Some have finials in the form of fruit on the lids which indicate their purpose. Covered sugar-bowls also had a slot in the lid for the perforated spoon, designed for sprinkling.

A popular form of sugar container in eighteenth-century England consisted of a cut-glass bowl set in a little pierced silver basket. These sugar-baskets were adopted in France and Italy from about 1770-80 onwards, when both countries experienced a wave of Anglomania. Italian silversmiths, especially those working in Piedmont and Genoa where a great deal of sugar was eaten,

◁ 235 Pair of sugar-casters with arms of the kings of Saxony, Augsburg, 1749/51, probably by Andreas Schneider, master silversmith 1738-85. Private collection.

236 Sugar-caster, Zurich, *c.* 1800, by Anton Manz, master silversmith from 1774 to after 1813. Private collection.

237 Sugar-bowl with a circle of spoons around a central spoon with a pierced bowl for sprinkling and a pointed handle for clearing the tea-pot spout, Zurich, *c.* 1740, by Sigmund Füessli, master silversmith 1712-50. Swiss National Museum, Zurich. LM 12485.

produced many sugar-tureens of very high quality. These Piedmontese and Genoese sugar containers were imitated by craftsmen in neighbouring parts of Europe—Savoy, Provence and southern Switzerland. Venetian silversmiths, on the other hand, continued to make the traditional uncovered sugar-bowls with little rests in the corners for sugar-spoons. A similar type of bowl was also produced in Switzerland and Germany. This had a central structure to hold the spoons, one of which had a pointed handle for clearing the tea-pot and a pierced bowl for sprinkling sugar.

The most popular form of sugar container in Portugal at the end of the eighteenth century was an urn-shaped bowl based on the English model. Various types were produced in Scandinavia. One which was popular in Sweden, the boat-shaped bowl, was based on a French design.

238 Design for a sugar container, Italy, *c.* 1780. Cooper-Hewitt Museum, New York. 1938-88-5570.

At the end of the eighteenth century a monumental silver object, obviously intended to form the centrepiece of the table, was made in France. The central container was surrounded by a circle of spoons arranged like a crown. This was clearly a sugar-bowl, but may also have been used as a container for jam.

Sugar was used on the Continent mainly in finely powdered form, but in English-speaking countries lump sugar was preferred, from 1680 onwards to sweeten tea, from 1690 for coffee, and from about 1700 for chocolate. In England sugar-bowls were made in the style of china rice-bowls. The bowls used in Ireland and America were bigger than their English counterparts. Extremely small sugar-bowls decorated with gadrooning were produced in

239 Covered sugar-bowl, Berne, *c.* 1810, by Georg Adam Rehfuss, master ▷ silversmith 1807-58. Musée de la Cathédrale, Lausanne.

170

171

240 Design for a sugar-bowl mounted on a tortoise, Italy, *c.* 1790. Cooper-Hewitt Museum, New York. 1938-88-4399.

241 Silver-gilt sugar-bowl, Paris, 1804, by Henry Auguste, master craftsman 1785-1816, based on drawings by Percier Fontaine. Musée de la Malmaison, Rueil.

242 Sugar container, Paris, *c.* 1800, by an unidentified master with the initials AHD. Musée de la Cathédrale, Lausanne.

Switzerland. Sugar-boxes similar to those for powder formed part of the luxurious toilet-sets produced by the silversmiths of Augsburg. These little boxes were equipped with locks, which shows how expensive sugar then was. Sugar-boxes, many of them of astonishingly high quality, were made by silversmiths wherever toilet-services were produced.

Sugar-tongs were invented in England, where lump sugar was favoured. The first ones were made in the form of scissors. Towards the middle of the eighteenth century they were simplified, becoming U-shaped with a grip at each end. Many different types of sugar-tongs have since been produced in almost every country, some of them quite fantastic.

The Mustard-Pot

Mustard is the popular name for the pungent sauce based on the seed of the mustard plant or *senapis*. The seed has to be crushed and reduced to a fine powder before it can be made into a sauce by adding vinegar, must or honey, according to taste. Mustard has always been very popular in northern Europe especially.

It has been used as a flavouring since the earliest times and, until the eighteenth century, was served at table in two different ways: as a powder or as a paste made from powder. Consequently containers and utensils are of different kinds. The cheaper domestic product was seldom served in silver receptacles before the seventeenth

243 Mustard-pot, Toulouse, 1756, by Antoine Mouset, master silversmith 1729-64. Metropolitan Museum of Art, New York. (Bequest of Catherine D. Wentworth, 1948.) 48.187.134.

244 Mustard-pot or *Sugerli*, Zurich, *c.* 1635, by Stefan Aaberli, master silversmith 1612-63. Swiss National Museum, Zurich. LM 469.

century. Silver was unsuitable as a container, since it is corroded by vinegar. Despite this, Louis XIV had several silver-gilt mustard containers, although they were probably dredgers for sprinkling mustard powder and therefore just like sugar-casters, but smaller. Similar receptacles were also made in England and Switzerland. Serving mustard in powder form disappeared during the eighteenth century, when it became more customary to serve it as a paste.

During the Middle Ages mustard was kept in little wooden or stone barrels which were placed on dressers. It was probably this tradition which led to the eighteenth-century practice of placing little barrel-shaped silver-gilt mustard-pots on magnificently arranged tables. These little kegs were sometimes fitted with

245 Pair of mustard-pots, Zurich, *c.* 1750, by Hans-Rudolf Manz, master silversmith 1734-72. Swiss National Museum, Zurich. Dep. 414 A and B.

handles. On Madame de Pompadour's luxurious table they were made to rest in cradles or wheelbarrows carried or pushed along by quaint little figures.

In English- and German-speaking countries a special form of mustard-pot was made. This was connected with the little keg-shaped container described above, but was in fact a cylindrical mug or tankard, smaller than the beer-tankard and provided with a spout for pouring mustard of weak consistency. This type remained in use throughout the eighteenth century and led to the development of

246 Mustard-pot, forming a pair with a matching sugar-caster, London, 1724, by Edward Gibbon. Colman Collection of Silver Mustard-Pots, Norwich.

247 Basket-shaped mustard-pot, London, 1856, by Robert Hennell III. Colman Collection of Silver Mustard-Pots, Norwich.

248 Mustard-pot, London, 1771, by Samuel Meriton I. Colman Collection of Silver Mustard-Pots, Norwich.

the characteristically English mustard-pot that is still the most popular form today. The body of the cylinder was very often pierced, revealing a blue cut-glass liner inside. As mustard gradually came to be served as a thicker paste, the spout was replaced by a slot to receive the ladle.

Some varieties of mustard-pot can hardly be distinguished from cream-jugs, since they followed the great diversification in shape which characterized the latter from the end of the seventeenth century until the nineteenth. The most certain way of recognizing these mustard-pots is by the aperture for the ladle or scoop.

The Tea-Caddy

Until the end of the nineteenth century, fashion required tea to be prepared by the mistress of the house herself in the presence of her guests. The traditional procedure followed in this ceremony, depicted in a number of illustrations, called for several silver utensils in addition to the tea-pot itself.

The most important of these was a container which was hermetically sealed so that the tea-leaves could be protected from light and damp and thus retain their volatile aroma and other qualities. Silver containers admirably fulfilled these requirements and were therefore used as soon as tea became a fashionable drink.

A magnificent tea-caddy was made by a Bruges silversmith at the beginning of the seventeenth century. This sumptuous article may

249   Tea-caddy, Ringkøbing, Denmark, 1729, by Jens Friis. Historiske Museum, Aalborg.

250   Tea-caddy, London, 1768, by Pierre Gillois, master silversmith from 1754. Museum of Fine Arts, Boston. 33.174.

251   Spice-box with screw-on lid, Augsburg, 1680, by Matthäus Messmer, ▷ master silversmith *c.* 1670-81. Private collection.

well have been a prototype of caddies made until the end of the following century. It is a piece of outstanding quality, basically oval in shape, but with a convoluted outline and flanked by caryatids. Its removable lid is dome-shaped. Later, rectangular caddies with lids that could be used to measure the tea were made in Flanders, the Netherlands, England and Denmark. The opening at the top was too small for easy refilling, but this difficulty was to some extent overcome by providing these caddies with sliding bottoms. Tea was not drunk in Germany until relatively late and china tea-caddies remained popular in that country. These were based on silver prototypes. Towards the mid-eighteenth century Swiss silver-smiths began to make oval, undulating or curved tea-caddies.

252 Design for a tea-caddy, Germany, *c.* 1750. Musée des Arts Décoratifs, Paris. CD 4284, fol. 132.

253 Tea-caddy, Basle, *c.* 1760, by Johann-Jacob Herzog, master silversmith 1745-95. Private collection.

Tea was more popular in England and America than anywhere else and craftsmen in those countries produced a great variety of caddies. From 1725 onwards they made caddies shaped like vases and urns richly adorned with rocaille work, of the kind featured in gardens of the period. The taste for the exotic in general and for chinoiserie in particular could be fully exploited in the tea-caddy, which was well suited to fantastic decoration of this sort. Tea was imported from China and the Indies in crates made of wooden boards, bound with cords and covered with labels and these details were often imitated in such engravings.

It became common to drink different varieties of tea according to the day of the week, the time of day, or the taste of the guests. This led, in England particularly, to the production of sets of caddies. There were usually three identical caddies in a set contained in a handsome wooden case covered with leather, tortoise-shell or mother-of-pearl. The word 'caddy', which only occurs in England, is derived from the Malay *kati*, a word used for a measure of tea. It has been suggested, but it is very unlikely, that the English word comes from the French *cadenas*, which was, as we have seen, the container in which kings and rulers locked away their salt, spices, etc. In these sets of three caddies, two usually contained two different kinds of tea and the third, which was generally bigger, lump sugar. Cylindrical tea-caddies were favoured in Scandinavia at a time when England and the Low Countries were under the influence of neo-classicism.

Finally, a word must be said about the spoons used for measuring tea. They were seldom made separately from caddies and are usually found attached to them. The bowls of such spoons were often of very original design, including scallop-shells or jockeys' caps.

The Centrepiece

As tables became larger, round, oval or oblong shapes grew more frequent; guests were more and more often seated all around these tables, so that the problem of what decoration to place in the middle arose. When the French form of service was followed, it became increasingly difficult to set out the dishes, tureens and covers, and the staff could not easily reach the centre. At fifteenth- and sixteenth-century banquets the middle of the table was adorned with a table-fountain, a monumental piece of silverware that would remain there throughout the meal. From the late seventeenth century onwards, craftsmen produced lasting works of art in silver as centrepieces for such great tables. They drew their inspiration

254 A centrepiece. Print based on J.-B. Oudry, taken from the *Fables* of La Fontaine, Paris, 1755. Private collection.

from earlier French and Italian banqueting-tables decorated with food, which was a perishable adornment. The practice of arranging food in pyramids supplied the model for the first centrepieces, which were known as *épergnes*. The *épergne* is unknown today in France, but the English version dating from about 1720 onwards is familiar; it consists basically of several baskets of various sizes fastened to a central frame.

According to the definition given in the *Cannaméliste Français* of 1768, the centrepiece is 'a silver machine placed in the centre of the

179

255 Design for a great centrepiece by Claude II Ballin (1661-1754), 1727/8. Musée des Arts Décoratifs, Paris. A 3625.

256 The silversmith Delaunay and the centrepiece that he made for the Dauphin, ▷ c. 1705. Detail of a portrait by Robert Tournières (1667-1752). Musée des Beaux-Arts, Caen.

table during all the courses; it is usually provided with oil-cruets, sugar-bowls or casters, lemons and other accessories'. Such centrepieces first appeared at the court of Versailles at the end of the seventeenth century. It was not long before other European courts followed the French example, as they seemed so useful. The centrepiece was known in Germany as a 'household dish'. French centrepieces always kept close to their original design and those who created them did not indulge in the fantasy that made

Augsburg silversmiths' centrepieces famous throughout Europe.

Most French centrepieces consisted of a slightly raised tray or salver on which the various receptacles for seasonings were arranged: salt-cellars, mustard-pots, sugar-casters, oil- and vinegar-cruets and boxes containing various spices. Branched candlesticks could also be added to provide lighting. A covered box or basket of fruit was placed in the middle. The fruit was surmounted by an ornamental structure which completed the decorative effect.

257   Design for a centrepiece, sugar-caster, cruet-stand for oil and vinegar and
spice-box, by Christian Precht, Sweden, *c.* 1740. Nationalmuseum, Stockholm.
NMH 677/1890 verso.

German centrepieces were influenced by contemporary ceramic objects and were much more imaginative. In addition to objects needed during the meal, they incorporated figurines, boskets, urns and pieces of trellis-work, together with other architectural features.

258   Design for a centrepiece with a central container, Paris, *c.* 1720. Kunst-bibliothek, Berlin (Staatliche Museen Preussischer Kulturbesitz). Hdz 3098.

259   Design for a centrepiece, Augsburg, mid-18th century. Musée des Arts Décoratifs, Paris. CD 4284, fol. 108.

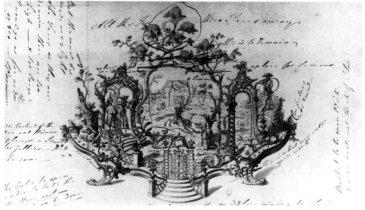

260   Design for a centrepiece, probably made by a French silversmith for a client in Russia, mid-18th century. Kunstbibliothek, Berlin (Staatliche Museen Preussischer Kulturbesitz). Hdz 3141.

261   Design for a centrepiece with notes and corrections made by an English organizer of banquets, Augsburg, mid-18th century. Musée des Arts Décoratifs, Paris. CD 4284, fol. 110.

262   Design for a tray used as table centrepiece, Italy, *c.* 1740. Cooper-Hewitt ▷ Museum, New York. 1938-88-8376.

263   Silver-gilt tray forming the base of a centrepiece, Augsburg, 1737/9, by ▷ Johann Heinrich Darjes, master silversmith 1733-1760. Private collection.

184

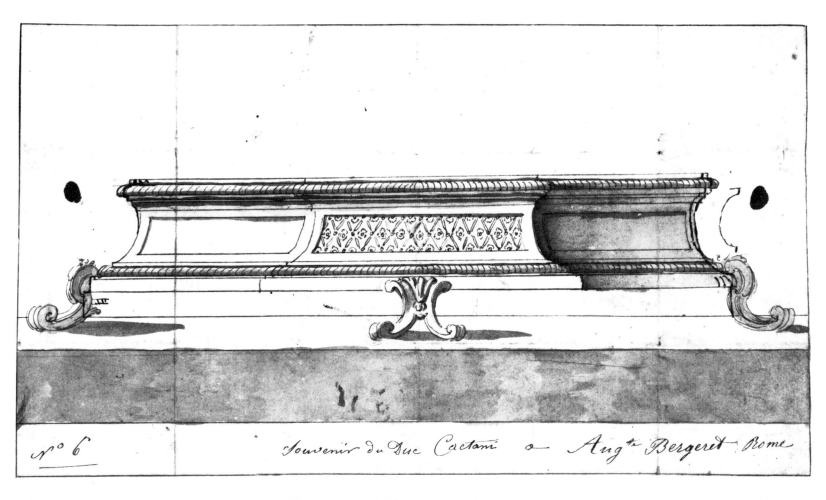

N° 6   Souvenir du Duc Cactani   &   Aug.te Bergeret Rome

◁ 264   Design for a table-runner consisting of mirrors in a silver frame, Germany, *c*. 1760. Musée des Arts Décoratifs, Paris. CD 4284, fol. 107.

◁ 265   Part of a table-runner and three baskets, supported by figures, forming a centrepiece, London, 1810, by Paul Storr. Private collection.

Oil- and Vinegar-Cruets

The centrepiece combined with a cruet-frame was confined to tables in the wealthiest homes. The more modest version is the silver oil and vinegar cruet-stand. This first appeared in France at the end of the seventeenth century. In its original form it consisted of a little tray containing pierced beakers, in which the glass cruets were placed. The frame could be lifted by a central handle on a stem. The stand was also equipped with holders for the silver

stoppers, which were replaced by glass stoppers when the oil and vinegar were served.

Under the Regency another kind of cruet-stand was made by French silversmiths. This consisted of a little uncovered tureen containing a structure consisting of several hoops within which the cruets and their stoppers could be placed. Towards the mid-eighteenth century both types of cruet-stand were combined in a boat-shaped vessel with a base-plate that was no longer removable. Centrepieces went out of fashion during the neo-classical period and oil- and vinegar-cruets became more important. They were often the only really decorative object on middle-class tables.

Although it originated in France, the cruet-stand quickly spread to other countries. Swedish craftsmen were directly inspired by French models. In Germany, the Netherlands, Italy and Switzerland open or covered salt-cellars were frequently mounted laterally on the base-plate. In England, where centrepieces were uncommon and the *épergne* was a feature of the short course served between the main dishes, sugar-casters, a mustard-pot and a pepper-caster were

266   Design for a cruet-stand, Paris, *c*. 1730, by Duplessis. Kunstbibliothek, Berlin (Staatliche Museen Preussischer Kulturbesitz). Hdz 3100.

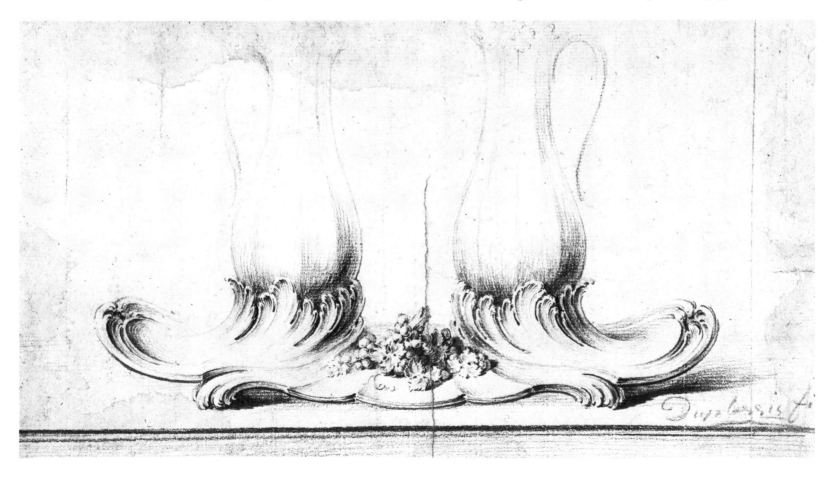

267 Cruet-stand with oil- and vinagar-cruets, Paris, 1779/80, by J.-L. Piccard, master silversmith 1778-81. Private collection.

268 Plan of a cruet-frame with a rocaille-work handle, possibly with lemóns; ▷ the salt consists of a silver-gilt leaf, Augsburg, mid-18th century. Musée des Arts Décoratifs, Paris. CD 4284.

A.

269

added to the oil- and vinegar-cruets when the French cruet-frame was adopted in 1720. These *épergnes* and cruet-frames had become very popular in England by the turn of the eighteenth to the nineteenth century.

269   Cruet-stand, Lausanne, *c.* 1795, by Antoine Pierre Mercier, mentioned 1791-1806. Private collection.

270   Design for a cruet-stand, Italy, *c.* 1750. Cooper-Hewitt Museum, New York. 1938-88-3193.

271   Design for a cruet-stand, Augsburg, *c.* 1810, by Johann Alois Seethaler, master craftsman 1796-1835. Cooper-Hewitt Museum, New York. 1911-28-339.

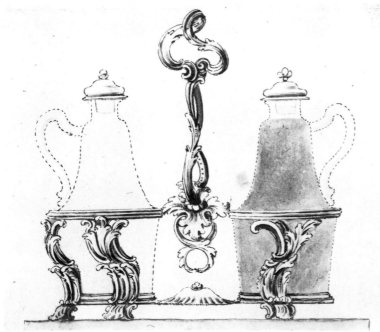

270

271

The Place Setting

The place setting or cover is nowadays limited to a knife, fork and spoon, but in the seventeenth century it also included a cloth, napkin and trencher or plate. From the end of the eighteenth century onwards, only the eating implements have formed part of the setting. All three were originally quite independent of each other and it was not until the second half of the eighteenth century that they became inseparable. The German word *Besteck*, which

originally meant the case or sheath into which personal cutlery and flatware were inserted, but which now simply refers to the knife, fork and spoon, points very clearly to the practice common at that time of combining these three implements in a personal container. These little cases formed the basis for the much larger canteens that

272   Table setting. Detail of damask table-cloth, by Paulus Jerma von Aachen, Copenhagen, 1622. Kremlin Treasury, Moscow.

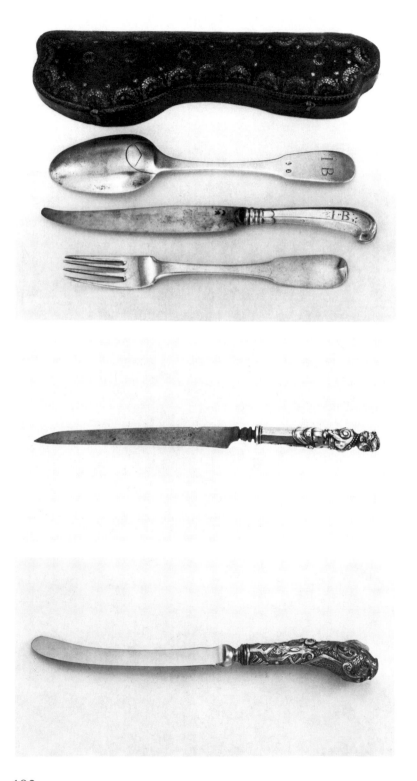

came into favour in the eighteenth century, in which a dozen or several dozen sets of cutlery and flatware were accommodated. These canteens were often made of precious metal.

The Knife

Of all the implements and objects used at table, the knife has undergone fewest changes of form and design. It consists of two main parts: blade and handle. The blade has always been made of metal, which may or may not have been precious. Until the eighteenth century the handle was made of many different materials, all of them hard and durable. Since the appearance of sets of cutlery and flatware, knife-handles have always been made to match those of forks and spoons.

The individual table knife first appeared in the fourteenth century. It was originally a much smaller version of the great carving-knife used by the staff in charge of cutting meat for those at table. After the Middle Ages the ceremony of carving survived only at royal or princely courts, or at meals marked by a special degree of solemnity. In houses where there was no servant who specialized in carving, the host and his guests themselves removed the bones from their meat with special hatchet-shaped knives. I have already mentioned, in connection with the silver sideboard in the Palazzo del Te, the little knives known as *parepains*. These were used for cutting a slice of bread, which was then placed on the wooden trencher and soaked up the gravy from the meat.

Gradually the knife was replaced for conveying meat to the mouth by the fork; the pointed tip disappeared and was replaced by a rounded end. By the sixteenth century, in Italy at least, the fork was already being widely employed, although pointed blades survived in France until the middle of the seventeenth century. They eventually disappeared as the result of the royal edicts promulgated by Cardinal Richelieu, who forbade knives to be used,

273 Travelling-case for a knife, fork and spoon, Basle, mid-18th century, by a silversmith belonging to the Fechter family. Private collection.

274 Knife with a herm handle, probably Venetian, late 16th century. Private collection.

275 Table knife with a pistol handle, Italy, late 17th century. Private collection.

276 Tortoise-shell canteen containing a dozen knives, forks and spoons, Lisbon, ▷ *c.* 1740, by an unidentified master with the initials LA. Fondação Ricardo Espirito Santo Silva, Lisbon.

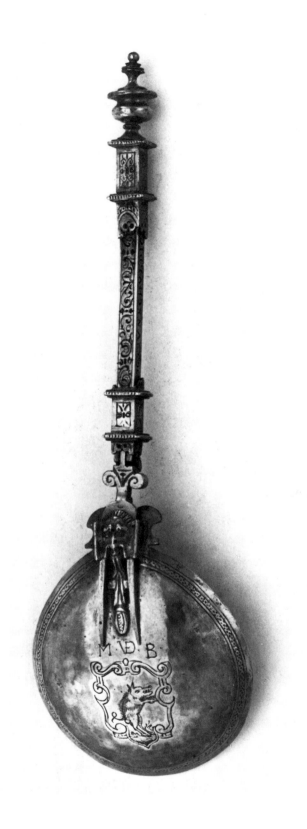

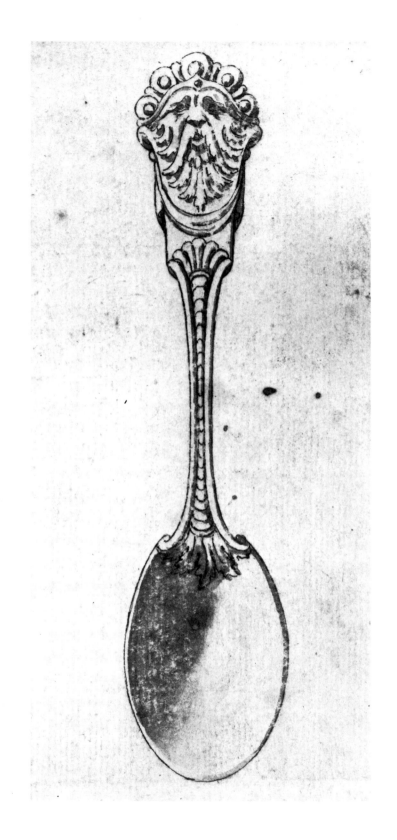

277 Spoon, the handle of which can be withdrawn to form a fork. Probably used by a prisoner, to judge from the words engraved on the handle: DVRCHAVS. VNSCHVLDICH / MACHT MICH GEDVLDICH. Augsburg (?), mid-17th century. No hallmarks. Private collection.

278 Drawing of a spoon, Italy, c. 1640. Cooper-Hewitt Museum, New York. 1938-88-5498.

279 Girl eating with a spoon from a bowl, by Francesco Fontebasso (1709-1768/9). Nationalmuseum, Stockholm. NM 85.

280 Spoon with octagonal handle, Paris, early 17th century. Private collection.

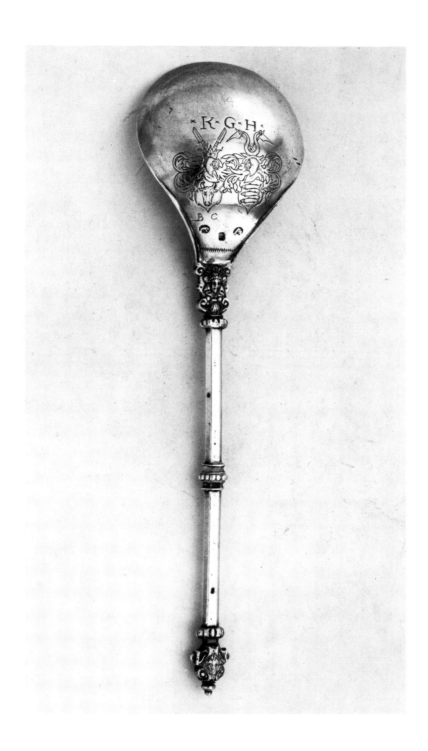

281 Spoon, Augsburg, *c.* 1600, by Abraham Schönauer, master silversmith before 1568-1614. Hallmarks of another town, possibly Schweidnitz, Silesia.

282 Spoon, Elbing, 1698, by Daniel Stahlenbrecher. Private collection.

283 Detail of a print of the feast given by the Spanish Ambassador in Paris to ▷ celebrate the birth of the Prince of the Asturias, 1717. The spoons are placed crossed on a pie; each guest has a knife and fork at his own place. Cabinet des Estampes, Bibliothèque Nationale, Paris.

284

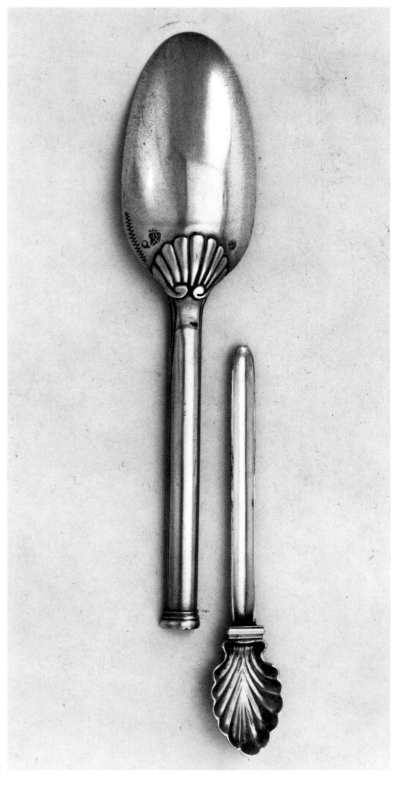

284 Case containing six silver-gilt coffee-spoons, Strasbourg, *c.* 1765, by Jacques-Henry Alberti, master silversmith 1764-95. Private collection.

285 Measuring spoon with a handle consisting of a little shell-shaped spoon and a spoon for extracting marrow, Dresden, 1741, by a master with the initials CDW (?). Private collection.

286 Little spoon and fork with a single handle, part of a travelling set of implements. The hallmarks are illegible, but are probably of Augsburg, late 17th century. Private collection.

285

286

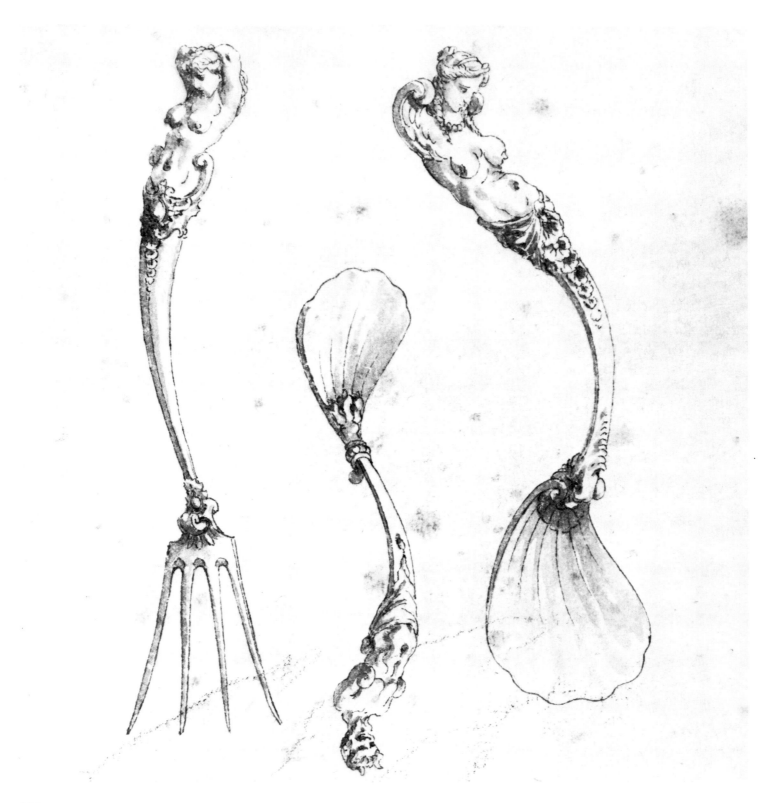

above all as tooth-picks. Even then many people must have continued to commit this social solecism since many knives still had a pointed end, although most now had rounded ones. In the second half of the seventeenth century, more and more straight or slightly curved blades were made, following the shape of the handle, which by that time almost always matched the handle of the fork.

The Spoon

From the earliest times until the end of the Middle Ages most spoons were carved from wood. Magnificent spoons have also been made of rock crystal or precious stones. Until quite recently the fork was a luxury article, but the spoon has always been an essential item and from the late Middle Ages onwards it has often been made of gold or silver, for reasons of hygiene. The spoon and beaker are the two silver objects most commonly found at all levels of society.

The late medieval spoon still resembled its prototype in antiquity. It had a short handle and a round, slightly concave bowl. As we have mentioned, towards the end of the sixteenth century,

◁ 287 Drawing of a set of Venetian cutlery, late 16th century. Cooper-Hewitt Museum, New York. 1938-88-7848.

288 Case for personal cutlery. Detail of a picture of Regula Rollenbutz of Zurich, 1583. Swiss National Museum, Zurich. LM 20990.

289 Knife and fork, probably from Venice, dated 1618. Swiss National Museum, Zurich. LM 55144/45.

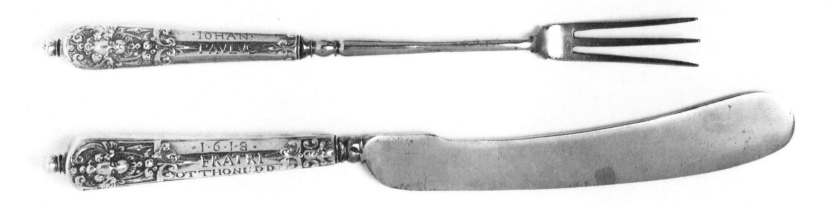

when great ruffs were commonly worn around the neck, the handle became longer, clearly to prevent the delicate lacework from being soiled. At the same time, the place where the bowl of the spoon joined the handle was strengthened by a 'rat's tail' and then, about 1630, the handle, which until then had been round or many-sided, was flattened to prevent the spoon from turning over.

The way in which spoons were decorated followed these changes in shape. The figurines, caryatids, fleurons and finials that used to adorn the ends of the curved handles disappeared. As the handle became flat, it either simply became wider at the end or else developed into the so-called *pied-de-biche* or trifid spoon. The handle itself might be elegantly moulded, violin-shaped, or adorned with engraving or lace-like chasing.

In addition to smaller spoons intended for personal use, others were made by silversmiths in varying sizes, according to the

◁ 290 A banquet in Fontainebleau Castle. A knight of the Holy Spirit can be seen eating with a fork. Detail of engraving by Abraham Bosse, 1633. British Library, London.

291 Fork and spoon of which the handles are entirely covered with engraved fruit and foliage, Zurich, *c.* 1700, by Dietrich Meyer, master silversmith 1675-1733. Swiss National Museum, Zurich. LM 10055 a, b.

292 *Le Bal à la Française*. Knives and forks can be seen on the right of the plates and a sugar-caster in the centre of the table. Detail of a print from the Almanach Royal, 1682. Cabinet des Estampes, Bibliothèque Nationale, Paris.

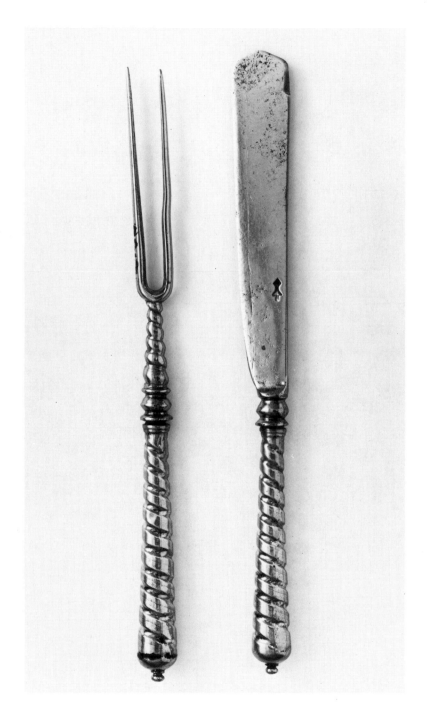

293 Knife and fork. The rounded blade of the knife ends in a little point. Zug, Switzerland, late 17th century. No hallmarks. Swiss National Museum, Zurich. LM 3405-118.

294 Matching knife and fork, Germany, late 17th century. Private collection.

295 Travelling set of flatware with articulated handles, consisting of a spoon and ▷ a fork together with a little marrow spoon and a tablet note-book, Augsburg, 1685/95, by Tobias Bauer, master silversmith 1685-1735. Private collection.

205

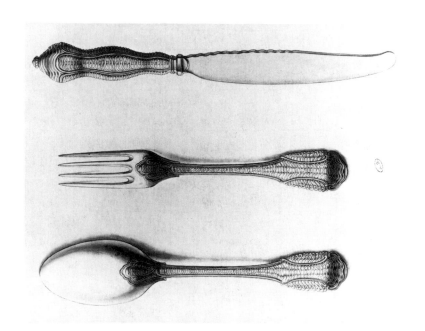

296 Design for a set of knife, fork and spoon with ripple handles, England, mid-18th century. Musée des Arts Décoratifs, Paris. CD 4284, fol. 153, Pl. 1.

297 Matching fork and spoon, Zug, Switzerland, *c*. 1740, by Franz Anton Hediger (1717-79). Private collection.

298 Design for a silver-gilt cutlery set consisting of a meat knife and fork with ▷ steel blade and prongs, a salt and marrow spoon, another knife and matching spoon, a spice-box and a knife (with a china handle), fork and spoon for the entremets course, Augsburg, *c*. 1760. Musée des Arts Décoratifs, Paris. CD 4284.

299 Matching knife, fork and spoon, forming part of a set, Strasbourg, *c*. 1760, ▷ by Jean-Louis II Imlin, master silversmith 1746-69. Private collection.

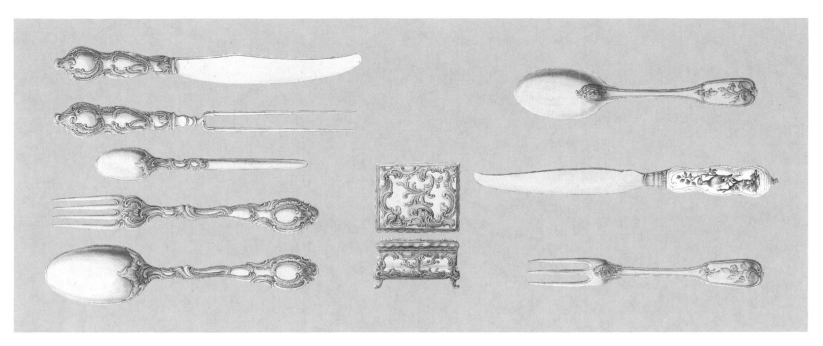

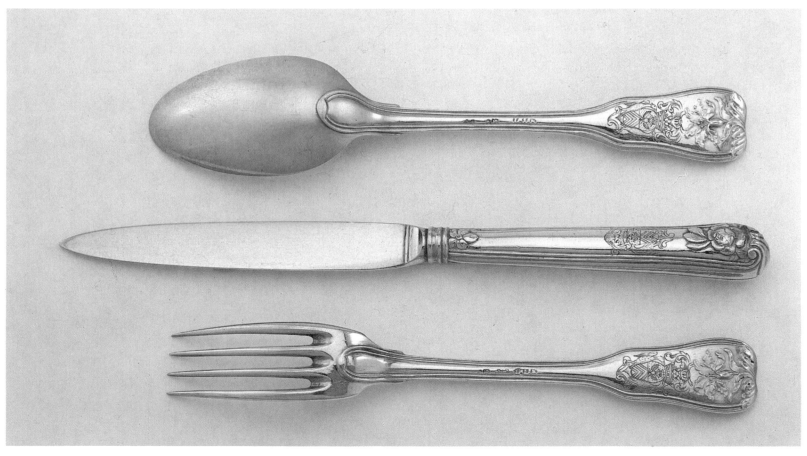

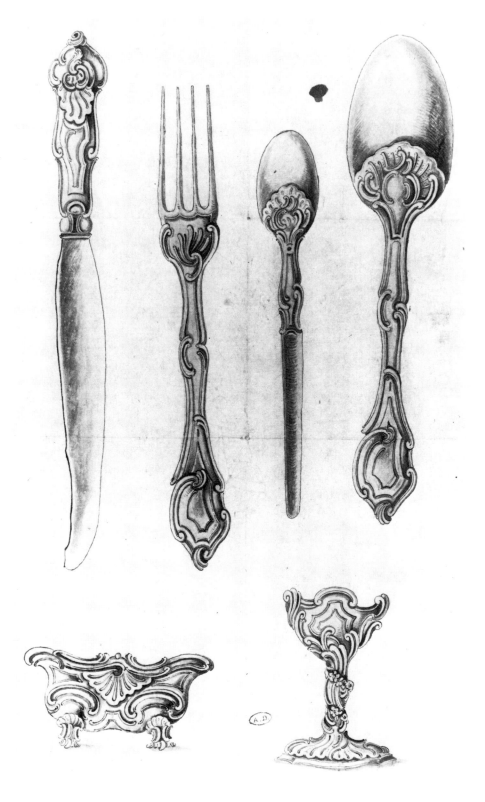

300 Design for a matching set of utensils consisting of a knife, fork and spoon, a salt and marrow spoon, an egg-cup and a spice-box, Augsburg, *c.* 1740. Musée des Arts Décoratifs, Paris. CD 4284, fol. 151, Pl. 1.

301 Set of convertible cutlery with different blades and forks, ▷ consisting of a knife, fork and spoon and a salt and marrow spoon, Dresden, probably 1754, by an unidentified master with the initials JGP. Private collection.

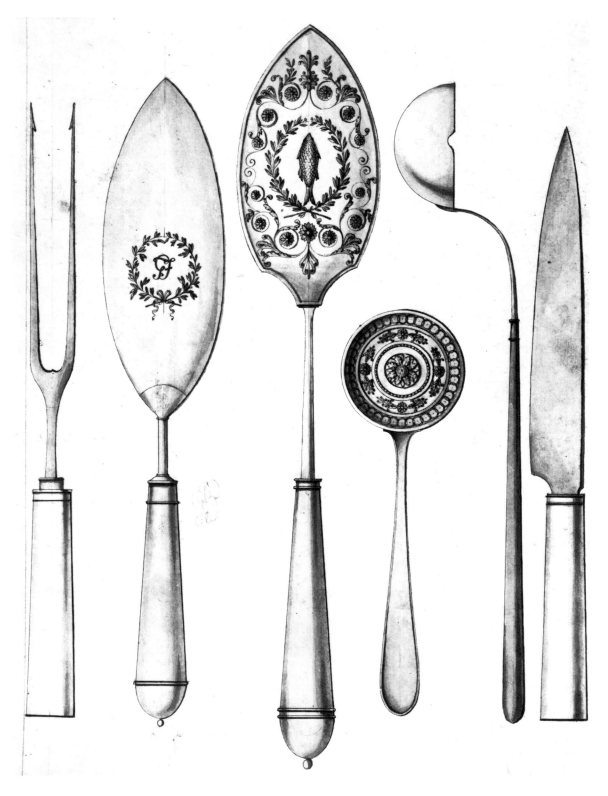

302 Design for a set of cutlery consisting of a carving fork, fish- and cake-slice, dredging-spoon, soup-ladle and knife, Italy, *c.* 1800, attributed to Giovacchino Belli, master silversmith 1787-1822. Cooper-Hewitt Museum, New York. 1938-88-5783.

303 Drawing of various sets of cutlery, Augsburg, mid-18th century. Musée des Arts Décoratifs, Paris. CD 4284, fol. 143. ▷

purpose they were to fulfil. Large serving spoons were, for example, very common from the end of the seventeenth century onwards. These are the biggest spoons known to us. Very small spoons were required for adding sugar to tea and coffee. Bone-marrow, a favourite dish, was eaten with a spoon that had a very long, oblong bowl. When broth-bowls were abandoned in favour of soup-tureens, the ladle was invented in Italy. Special ladles for sauces and punch, olive-spoons, perforated spoons, strainers and ice- and salt-scoops were all derived from the simple spoon described above.

The Fork

The individual fork used to convey food to the mouth is a very small version of the kitchen fork known to the ancients, but its original form is not known. According to St. Bonaventure, it was introduced to Venetian society in the mid-eleventh century by the Byzantine princess who married the Doge of Venice, Domenico Silvio. This early type of fork had two short prongs. It was clearly a magnificent object and its presence is recorded by chance in medieval inventories.

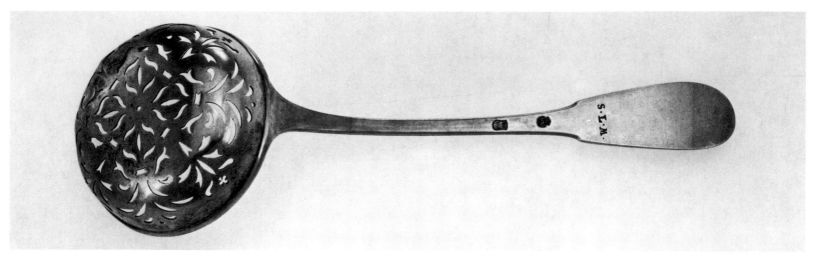

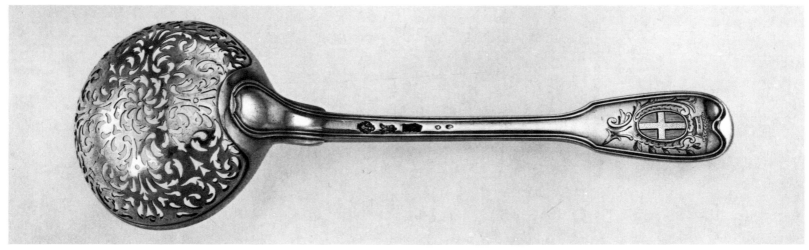

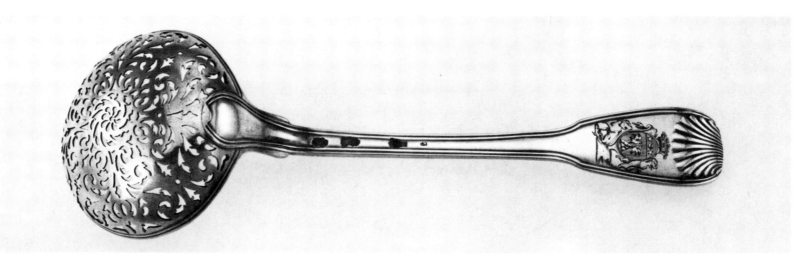

We have to wait until the Italian Renaissance before we find ladies beginning to use little forks to eat fruit and delicacies without staining their fingers. This refinement was for a long time practised only by courtesans, which accounts for the Church's ban on the fork as an implement associated with immorality. According to legend, Henry III became infatuated with the fork when he went to Venice and subsequently introduced it to the French court. Gentlemen invited by Louis XIII to a meal in honour of the Order of the Holy Spirit can be seen using forks in an engraving by Abraham Bosse.

The fork did not appear in England until later. An English visitor to Italy in 1617 was astonished to see forks being used. He concluded that this must be because the Italians were so dirty! The first English fork has been dated to 1632. Switzerland was influenced by Venice and already had forks at the beginning of the seventeenth century. By the middle of the same century, the Swiss were completely at home with them. At that time the handles of Swiss forks were decorated in the same way as their spoons.

The use of the fork remained a bone of contention for a long time in France. In about 1690, Louis XIV criticized the governess of the little Duke of Burgundy and his brothers for teaching them to eat with a fork instead of with their fingers like all well brought-up people! Yet around 1710 the fork suddenly became widely used.

In German-speaking countries two kinds of fork co-existed throughout the eighteenth century. The first had two long steel prongs and was designed especially for eating meat. The second had four or five prongs which formed a single unit with the handle, of silver or silver-gilt. This fork was made according to the French model.

It is very difficult to establish an accurate chronology of the development of the fork and the number of its prongs, since it is precisely here that the habits in each region have been so different. As with the knife and spoon, one may observe a change in the decoration of fork-handles as styles were modified in each country.

307 Fish-slice, Germany, *c.* 1730, by an unidentified master with the initials ICH. Private collection.

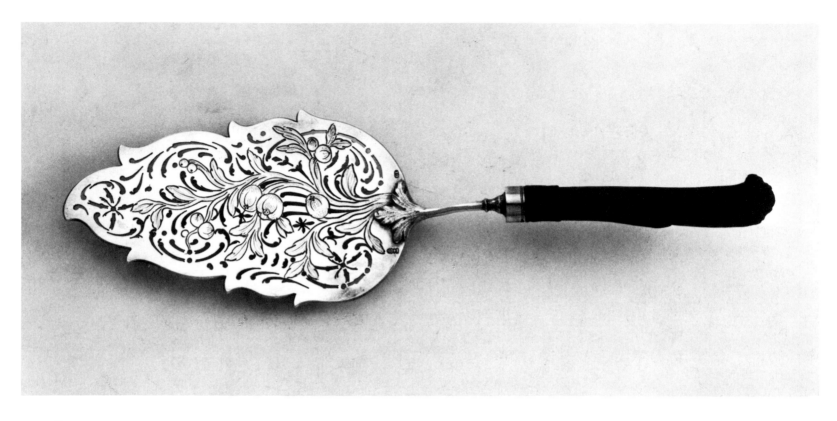

214

308 Cake-slice, Augsburg, 1779/81, by Gottfried Lütkers, master silversmith 1756-86. Private collection.

309 Fish-slice, Lausanne, *c.* 1820, by F. Lecomte (1788-1861). Swiss National Museum, Zurich. LM 52465.

310 Cadenas, The Hague, 1616, by Jan G. Osterlingh. Rijksmuseum, Amsterdam.

The Cadenas

The cadenas is the more modern version of the medieval nef, in which certain foods and accessories belonging to the ruler were locked away to avoid the risk of poison. Because it was the property of a royal personage, it was always made of precious metal. Two kinds of cadenas existed simultaneously in all the courts of Europe. The first was fundamentally a rectangular casket, richly decorated, mounted on four little feet, and provided with a knob. The second

type was more common. It consisted of a square or rectangular plate or tray with a set of compartments on one side or at one end. These compartments were either open or covered and contained the sovereign's cutlery, salt, spices and bread. The tray was for his napkin, which was presented to him at the beginning of the meal.

Cadenas of this second type were already being made in the sixteenth century. Henry II of France had one on his table and the Cardinal of Sens had one in Italy, where it was seen by Michel de

311 Silver-gilt cadenas belonging to the Empress Joséphine, Paris, 1804, by Henry Auguste, master silversmith 1785-1816. The maker followed drawings by Percier and Fontaine. Musée de la Malmaison, Rueil. 47.268.

Montaigne in 1581. In the seventeenth century there were cadenas at all the courts of Europe, but it would seem that, in the era of Louis XIV, it appeared on the sovereign's table more as a royal symbol than as a functional object. Louis gave away magnificent cadenas as a sign of royal favour or personal affection, both to members of his own family and foreign sovereigns. The King of England had a cadenas on his table in 1683 and Charles X of Sweden received two as gifts from the King of France. The silversmiths of Dresden, a very important centre of luxurious silverware in the eighteenth century, made cadenas for the court of Saxony and Poland. Napoleon I also had cadenas on his table.

Fruit- or Bread-Baskets

English craftsmen invented the silver basket to contain fruit or bread, based on the delicate wickerwork produced there. The first silver baskets were made in the seventeenth century. They were round and pierced with decorative themes in the contemporary style. An excellent example has been dated to 1656. It is richly adorned with realistic flowers and fruit and was no doubt greatly valued.

Paul de Lamerie, the famous London silversmith, evolved a particularly elegant and finely wrought oval-shaped basket with one handle or two grips. The type with the single handle could be passed easily from one person at table to another, whereas the second type could be used as a decorative centrepiece. Pyramids of fruit were the traditional way of ornamenting tables in the seventeenth century and Paul de Lamerie's basket was clearly in accordance with that tradition; at the same time it anticipated the arrival in England of the typical eighteenth-century table centre-piece. These consisted either of a single central basket or several of them placed one above the other, surrounded by a number of suspended miniature baskets. This form of centrepiece was, as we have already seen, known in England as the *épergne*.

Very many openwork silver baskets were made in the Low Countries in the eighteenth century. Until about 1775 silversmiths there produced some remarkable masterpieces of rocaille work, thus clearly following their own tradition in the decorative arts that reached a peak about 1640. Dutch baskets always have grips at the sides.

Around 1745 a basket in the shape of a great shell with a single curved handle became fashionable in Britain. Its popularity

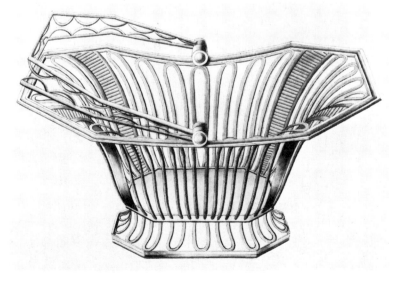

312   Bread-basket, Lausanne, *c.* 1815, by Marc and Charles Gély, known as the Gély brothers, 1813-46. Private collection.

313   Design for a bread-basket, Augsburg, *c.* 1810, probably by J.A. Seethaler, master silversmith 1796-1835. Cooper-Hewitt Museum, New York. 1911-28-348.

314 Bread-basket, London, mid-18th century, by Benjamin Godfrey. Museum of Fine Arts, Boston. (Theodora Wilbour Fund.) 60.946.

315 Bread-basket, Augsburg, 1803, by Johann Christian Neuss, master silver- ▷ smith 1766-1803. Private collection.

219

continued well into the following century. Since the end of the eighteenth century, silver baskets have been used less for fruit than for bread and have also become much more common. Fruit came to be offered instead in baskets of gilded bronze or china which formed part of the table-runner. Very many different forms of basket were created in England in that period, most of them decorated in very delicate openwork. German, Swiss and Austrian silversmiths produced excellent imitations of these English silver baskets.

Wine-Coolers, Monteiths, Wine-Glass Coolers and Portable Cellars

The problem of supplying cool drinks in the heat of summer was solved in the past by a complicated system of ice-boxes. Ice was gathered in the winter and stored in caves. It was a luxury commodity and was presented at table in sumptuous ice-boxes, which were usually made of metal so that the ice would not melt so easily. In more wealthy homes these ice-boxes were made of silver. There were two basic forms: the wine-cooler for bottles and the wine-glass cooler.

In medieval illustrations a great vat or bucket with two handles can often be seen resting on the floor, filled with flagons, bottles and pots kept in ice. These cooling-buckets were first made of precious metal in the seventeenth century. Very few, however, have escaped the melting-pot. They may have been introduced into France by Cardinal Mazarin, but those that have survived are now confined to England.

During the second half of the seventeenth century, when it was common to display silverware on great buffets and dressers, smaller vases were used as wine-coolers for one or two bottles. These have all disappeared, but several imitations of them exist in china, so that we have a good idea of their form and ornamentation. They are usually urn-shaped and have a hollow lid with a central knob; this lid can also be used as a cooling bowl. Several French examples dating back to the eighteenth century have been preserved in Portugal, Germany, Russia and Sweden.

A distinctive form of wine-cooler or wine-glass cooler was developed in England. This is the Monteith, which can usually be distinguished by its removable upper rim, which was normally scalloped or notched. One of the first may be dated to 1683. The Monteith was apparently named after a noble Scot who wore a notched cloak. Wine-bottles could be kept cool in it and, when its notched rim was in place, wine-glasses could be held in the notches

and kept cool in the ice. Wine-coolers went out of fashion at the beginning of the eighteenth century, but they became popular again during the neo-classical period, when they were made in the form of ancient kraters. We have encountered such wine-coolers at two of the occasions illustrated in the first part of this book.

A French form of wine-glass cooler was developed at the same time as the Monteith. Many specimens were produced during the eighteenth century. This oval container with two handles has a notched rim, similar to that of the Monteith, for holding glasses with stems. From the beginning of the nineteenth century it became normal to place wine-glasses on the table. This marked the end of the Monteith and its French counterpart, which were, from then onwards, used as *jardinières*.

316 Silver-gilt wine-cooler, part of the Great Gilded Silverware of the Anointing, Paris, 1804, by Henry Auguste, master silversmith 1785-1816, based on the design by Percier, Fontaine. Musée de la Malmaison, Rueil. 47.277/278.

317 Silver canteen or portable cellar, Paris, 1712/13, by Claude II Ballin, ▷ master silversmith 1661-1754. Silberkammer der Residenz, Munich.

221

318 Wine-cooler, forming part of the Kharkov service at St. Petersburg, Augsburg, 1781/3, by Johann Christian Neuss, master silversmith 1766-1803. Private collection.

Louis XIV enjoyed great luxury when he went to war. One article which accompanied him on his campaigns was a metal canteen in which food was kept at a suitable temperature. These portable cellars were also used to transport bottles of wine at the right temperature for drinking. Silver portable cellars or canteens were also used, as we have already seen, to keep food warm during great meals held in halls which were a long way from the kitchens.

319 Monteith, Dublin, 1726, by Thomas Sutton. Ulster Museum, Belfast.

320 Design for a cooler for bottles and flagons of wine, Rome, second quarter of 18th century. Cooper-Hewitt Museum, New York. 1938-88-8232.

322   Drawing of a Monteith, Augsburg, mid-18th century. Musée des Arts ▷
Décoratifs, Paris. CD 4284, fol. 32.

321   Monteith, England, *c.* 1707, by John Leach. Museum of Fine Arts, Boston.
(Theodora Wilbour Fund.) 40.191.

323   Monteith, London, *c.* 1725, by Paul de Lamerie. Museum of Fine Arts, ▷
Boston. (Theodora Wilbour Fund.) 55.460.

324 Design for a wine-cooler, Germany, mid-18th century. Musée des Arts
Décoratifs, Paris. DC 4284, fol. 94.

The Dish-Ring or Stand and the Lamp

When the French form of service at table was followed, the dish-ring or stand was an indispensable item to prevent the table from being damaged by hot dishes. It went out of favour at the beginning of the nineteenth century when meals ceased to be served in the French way, although it survived to some extent in England and above all in Ireland. The earliest English examples date back to the reign of Queen Anne. They were very quickly adopted in Ireland and remained popular until well into the nineteenth century. They were decorated attractively in openwork with a variety of themes, and so made a fine impression on the table. Their sides were sometimes straight and sometimes widened out at the top and bottom.

325　Dish-ring, Dublin, 1770, by Christopher Hawes. Metropolitan Museum of Art, New York. (Gift of Irwin Untermyer, 1968.) 68.141.78.

Lamps have existed in every country in Europe and at all periods. Although it did not appear until the seventeenth century, the most frequent type in silver was a basin-shaped lamp with a pierced upper part, mounted on feet, fitted with a straight, turned handle made of wood and containing embers in its lower well. The shape of such lamps changed according to the use to which they were put.

326 Lamp heated by embers on the table. Detail of print by Abraham Bosse (1602-76). Cabinet des Estampes, Bibliothèque Nationale, Paris.

327 Drawing of a lamp heated by embers or a brazier, Rome, *c.* 1725. ▷ Cooper-Hewitt Museum, New York. 1938-88-8102.

328 Lamp heated by embers, London, *c.* 1706, by Anthony Nelme. Museum ▷ of Fine Arts, Boston. (Gift of Mrs Charlotte Beebee Wilbour.) 39.20.

228

Souvenir du Duc Caetani — Augte. Bergeret) Rome

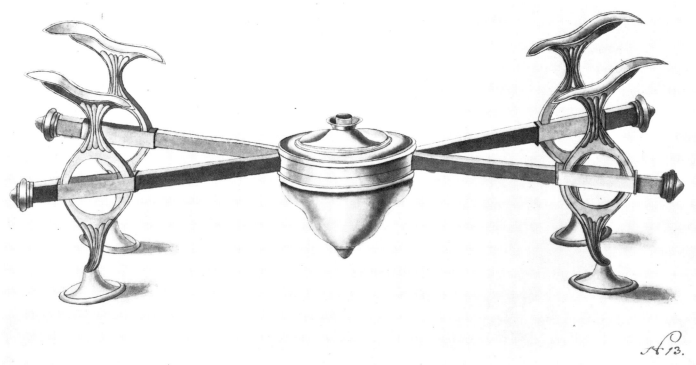

A.13.

Another type of lamp was heated by spirits. This became very popular in the eighteenth century, when it was almost always made of silvered brass. The French form of spirit-lamp consists of a ring resting on three feet which have an extension at the top consisting of hinged tongues, thus making it possible for very large dishes to be placed on them. This type of lamp also has a straight wooden handle. The spirit-burner is suspended inside the ring. A number of variants exist. They are usually more elaborate and sometimes form part of sets consisting of a kettle and a tea- or coffee-pot, all of which have flat bottoms.

Sometimes lamps are incorporated into large silver receptacles such as hot-water urns and Russian samovars, in which the water is heated inside the container by hot coals in tubes. Towards the middle of the eighteenth century, a very ingenious lamp was invented in England to heat dishes of different sizes. The spirit-lamp was fixed in the centre of a cross, the arms of which could be extended or made smaller. Some time later, around 1800, egg-boilers provided with spirit-lamps were made in France, Switzerland and the Netherlands, so that eggs could be prepared at the serving-table.

331   Little spirit-lamp, Paris, 1788. Maker's marks illegible. Private collection.

◁ 329   Lamp heated by embers, France, *c.* 1720. No hallmarks. Metropolitan Museum of Art, New York. (Bequest of Catherine D. Wentworth, 1948.) 48.187.76.

◁ 330   Design for a dish-stand with extending arms and a little spirit-lamp, Augsburg, *c.* 1800, by Johann Alois Seethaler, master silversmith 1796-1835. Cooper-Hewitt Museum, New York. 1911-28-347.

The House

Braziers and Foot-Warmers

The brazier or *brasero* originated in Spain and was introduced into France in the seventeenth century, when as we know there was close contact between the two countries. Silver had seldom been used before the reign of Louis XIV, but braziers made of this precious metal were used at his court in an attempt to warm the

great rooms of his castles. They were forbidden outside the court, however, and even those belonging to the court were melted down at the end of the Sun King's reign.

The only ones to survive were very small braziers used as foot-warmers. These usually consist of a container for the embers, which may be of various shapes, a pierced lid and a large wooden handle. They were made in Italy and France throughout the eighteenth and nineteenth centuries.

332 Three drawings of foot-warmers, Rome, *c.* 1810, by Giovacchino Belli, master silversmith 1787-1822, or his son Pietro Belli, master 1825-8. Cooper-Hewitt Museum, New York. 1938-88-5782.

333 Foot-warmer, Bologna (?), *c.* 1725, by an unknown master. Kunstgewer- ▷ bemuseum, Berlin (Staatliche Museen Preussischer Kulturbesitz). 02.75.

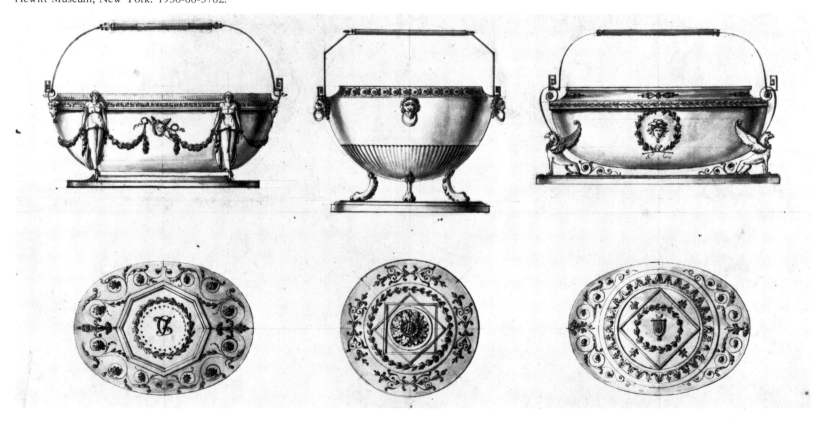

232

334 Foot-warmer, Austria (?), *c.* 1780. No hallmarks. Private collection.

Means of Lighting

The Chamber Candlestick

Although the chamber candlestick *(bougeoir)* must have been known before the Renaissance, the name itself, as applied to the smallest source of domestic lighting, first appeared at the beginning of the sixteenth century. This form of hand-held candlestick was used mainly to light one's way in a dark house. Its use became widespread at all levels of society; this occurred quite rapidly as wax rather than tallow came to be employed for candles.

Chamber candlesticks could be made of any metal, but silver, as we know, had the great advantage of reflecting the flame of the candle and thus doubling the strength of the light. Because it was small, relatively light in weight and therefore not too expensive, the candlestick was one of the commonest silver objects until the nineteenth century. In addition to this, its shape, which was designed to make it easily carried, has hardly changed since the

seventeenth century. It consists of a tray with a central socket to hold the candle. It also has a handle, a tail or a ring so that it can be carried. It is, moreover, hardly possible for such a very simple basic structure to be decorated in a great variety of ways, with the result that in this respect too there were hardly any changes either in France or in England until the end of the nineteenth century.

During the seventeenth century, the chamber candlestick was an element in the ceremonial when the king retired to bed at the courts of Louis XIII and Louis XIV. In the latter's household especially it was regarded as a great honour to carry the king's candlestick, which was distinguished by its two drip-receivers; only those courtiers closest to the monarch were permitted to perform this task. None of these candlesticks for two candles has, unfortunately, survived.

Another type, which may have been used exclusively in church, had a long hollow cylindrical handle which could hold a spare candle. Very ornate specimens were made until the beginning of the nineteenth century.

The candlestick, being so common, has given rise to many customs in different countries and at different times. For example, a lighted candlestick set in front of a guest's place at table would indicate discreetly that a bed was available for him for the night.

335 Chamber candlestick, Bordeaux, 1760/2, by David Herbert, master silver-smith 1747-71. Metropolitan Museum of Art, New York. (Bequest of Catherine D. Wentworth, 1948.) 48.187.54.

Chamber candlesticks have almost always been accompanied by candle-snuffers or douters to extinguish the flame of the candle. Sometimes this snuffer is found attached by a little chain to the candlestick; in other cases it is either placed on a cone at the end of the handle or fixed to the edge of the pan. There are also many examples of snuffers existing independently, for instance in the silver collection of Louis XIV.

A miniature English version of the candlestick is known as the taperstick. The tiny flame of the taper was often used in the

336 Chamber candlestick, Dijon, *c.* 1725, by an unidentified master with the initials PD (Pierre Dumont?). Musée des Arts Décoratifs, Paris. 30.154.

337 Pair of candlesticks known as *ménagères*, Berne, 1805, by Ludwig Friedrich Brugger, mentioned 1803-10. Swiss National Museum, Zurich. LM 24344/5.

eighteenth century to melt sealing-wax. Logically, tapersticks are almost always associated with inkstands.

A candlestick that was produced in considerable numbers in France and Switzerland in the eighteenth and early nineteenth centuries is known as the *ménagère* ('housekeeper'). It is halfway between a chamber candlestick and a candlestick with a column. It often replaced the chamber candlestick as a means of finding one's way around the house. It consists of a pan and a cylindrical foot with slots at regular intervals so that the candle inside could be pushed up as it burned down. In this way there was no danger of the candle burning away completely or of it falling to the ground.

The Table Candlestick

According to Richelet, the table candlestick (*flambeau*) 'consists of a mouthpiece into which the candle is inserted, a pipe and a foot, which is usually fashioned and embellished'. Working from these three essential elements, seventeenth- and eighteenth-century silversmiths made this magnificent object reflect perfectly all the successive styles in vogue during those two hundred years. The candlestick was an indispensable source of light for the dining- and

toilet-table and an essential element of decoration in the home. At night one could not live without it.

From the Middle Ages onwards craftsmen in Flanders and the Netherlands specialized in making bronze candlesticks, and their work inspired silversmiths. Works made of bronze had always been popular in northern Italy, so that bronze candlesticks, too, were favoured for a long time there; it was not until the eighteenth century that silver candlesticks appeared as household furnishings.

In the seventeenth century Dutch silversmiths continued to base their work on a prototype which had a very large foot or base, shaped like a salt-cellar, and a simple cylindrical stem with a socket at the top. The same basic type of candlestick was also made in England, but it was richly adorned with floral themes and foliated scrolls in repoussé chasing. About 1635 French craftsmen began to produce a type with fluted pilasters and a square base, which proved to be very successful outside France as well for a very long time. In northern Europe the earlier form was made very much richer and heavier with Baroque decoration. Pilasters were rejected in favour of twisted columns, richly worked and overburdened with floral and vegetable themes. The pillar candlestick, which returned to fashion again and again until the beginning of the twentieth

338 Pair of candlesticks, London, *c.* 1643/50, by A. Moore (?). Museum of Fine Arts, Boston. (Theodora Wilbour Fund.) 67.602.3.

339 Pair of candlesticks. Boston, *c.* 1695/1700, by the silversmith Noyes (1674-1749). Museum of Fine Arts, Boston. (Gift of Miss Clara Bowdoin.)

238

340 Pair of large candlesticks, Augsburg, *c.* 1695/1700, by Johann I Mittnacht, master silversmith 1671-1727. Private collection.

341 Candelabrum, Stockholm, 1718, by Jacob Brunck, master silversmith 1715-43. Maria Kyrka, Stockholm.

342 Candlestick, Delft, 1652, by Willem C. Brugman. Rijksmuseum, Amsterdam.

343

344

345

346

343   Pair of large silver-gilt candlesticks, Breslau (Wrocław), late 17th century, by an unidentified master with the initials AVN. Private collection.

344   Candlestick, Stockholm, 1713, by Johan Bress, master silversmith 1702-16. Nationalmuseum, Stockholm.

345   Candlestick, Copenhagen, 1702, by Gerhard Weghorst. Kunstindustrimuseet, Copenhagen. 12 A/1950.

346   Little candlestick on a writing-table, from a portrait of *Madame de Pompadour*, by François Boucher, *c.* 1750. Repository of the Bayerische Hypotheken- und Wechsel-Bank, Alte Pinakothek, Munich.

century, also originated in France. England adopted it in the seventeenth century and remained faithful to it for two centuries.

The candlestick with a baluster-shaped stem, a triangular base and a pricket rather than a nozzle for the candle itself can be traced back to antiquity. It survived until the nineteenth century on church altars. From the seventeenth century onwards, it became popular in secular society, too, the pricket being replaced by a socket and the shape of the base varying. In England the stem often resembled the turned legs of furniture of the period, while in France different baluster stems co-existed. Around 1680 the commonest form of base was square with cut surfaces. This survived throughout the eighteenth century with only very slight changes.

347   Design for four-branched candelabrum for Louis XV's service, attributed to Thomas Germain, *c.* 1730. Cooper-Hewitt Museum, New York. 1911-28-274.

348   Design for a three-branched candlestick, Germany, *c.* 1730. Musée des Arts Décoratifs, Paris. CD 4284, fol. 48.

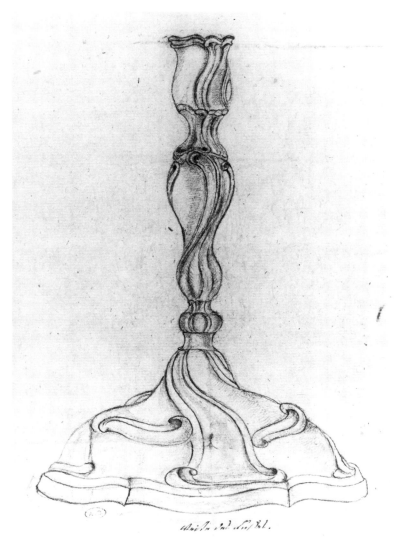

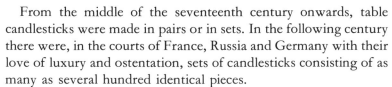

349 Design for a candlestick, Germany, *c.* 1750. Musée des Arts Décoratifs, Paris. CD 4284, fol. 35.

350 Design for a three-branched candelabrum, Augsburg, *c.* 1740. Musée des Arts Décoratifs, Paris. CD 4284, fol. 46.

From the middle of the seventeenth century onwards, table candlesticks were made in pairs or in sets. In the following century there were, in the courts of France, Russia and Germany with their love of luxury and ostentation, sets of candlesticks consisting of as many as several hundred identical pieces.

Many different styles in striking contrast to each other were developed in the eighteenth century—the severe classical style, for example, was followed by a taste for rocaille work with its tortured shapes and then by neo-classicism—with the result that table candlesticks were made in an almost infinite variety of forms. In

351 Design for a two-branched candlestick, Germany, *c.* 1750. Musée des Arts Décoratifs, Paris. CD 4284, fol. 41.

352 Design for a rocaille-work candlestick, Germany, *c.* 1740. Musée des Arts Décoratifs, Paris. CD 4284, fol. 29.

353 Drawing of five-branched candlestick, Germany, *c.* 1750. Musée des Arts Décoratifs, Paris. CD 4284, fol. 44.

242

351

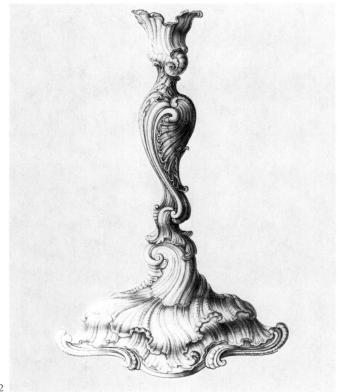

352

353

244

◁ 354 *Le Retour du bal*. A candlestick can be seen on the little table. Print by Beauvarlet, based on J.F. de Troy, mid-18th century. Cabinet des Estampes, Bibliothèque Nationale, Paris.

355 Pair of candlesticks from the collection of King Augustus III of Saxony, engraved with his monogram, Dresden, *c.* 1745, by Christian Heinrich Ingermann, master silversmith 1732-71. Private collection.

356 Pair of candlesticks, Paris, 1763/4, by Louis-Joseph Lenhendrick, master silversmith 1747-83. Private collection.

357

358

359

357 Candlestick, Stockholm, 1774, by Lars Boye, master silversmith 1762-95. Nordiska Museet, Stockholm.

358 Candlestick, Göteborg, 1782, by Andreas Reutz, master silversmith 1767-1810. Nordiska Museet, Stockholm.

359 Pair of 'trumpet' candlesticks, Lausanne, 1750, by Philibert Potin, mentioned 1740-82. Private collection.

360 Design for four-branched candelabrum, Augsburg, *c.* 1800, by Johann Alois Seethaler, master silversmith 1796-1835. Cooper-Hewitt Museum, New York. 1911-28-311.

361 Design for three candlesticks, Rome, *c.* 1810, by Pietro Belli, master silversmith 1825-8. Cooper-Hewitt Museum, New York. 1938-88-5794.

362 Candlestick, Stockholm, 1822, by Erik Adolf Zethelius, master silversmith 1803-39. Nordiska Museet, Stockholm.

360

361

362

247

England, the pillar type continued to be popular, but as many specimens were made there with baluster stems cut in facets and mounted on polygonal bases or with circular and highly ornamented baluster stems based on the French model.

In France the baluster candlestick became more popular than all other forms towards the end of the seventeenth and throughout the eighteenth centuries. Year after year saw the production of beautiful examples with convoluted, moulded, fluted or gadrooned stems and bases; sometimes they were decorated with grotesques and other themes taken from sculpture and architecture. Candlesticks were also successfully decorated with rocaille work, although this fashion persisted only in Germany and northern Italy. An original trumpet-shaped candlestick became fashionable in Berne and French-speaking Switzerland, Italy, Portugal and Flanders.

363   Drawing of silver chandelier. Paris, *c.* 1700. Part of the Tessin collection. Nationalmuseum, Stockholm. THC 862.

364   Candelabrum arm, Utrecht, 1647, by Michiel de Bruyn van Berendrecht. ▷ Boymans-van Beuningen Museum, Rotterdam. B. 2.16/17.

365 Sconce with reflecting plate, London, 1700, by Joseph Ward. Metropolitan Museum of Art, New York. (Gift of Irwin Untermyer, 1968.) 68.141.53.

366 Sconce for a single candle, London, 1709/10, by John Jackson. Museum of Fine Arts, Boston. (Theodora Wilbour Fund.) 63.784-5.

367 Drawing of a silver candelabrum arm, Germany, mid-18th century. Musée des Arts Décoratifs, Paris. CD 4284, fol. 36.

Towards the middle of the eighteenth century an extremely contorted form of candlestick was evolved by German silversmiths, those of Augsburg and Dresden in particular. This type remained fashionable all over central Europe until the end of the century. These playful forms did not lose their appeal even when neo-classical designs achieved such success in Germany, the Netherlands and Scandinavia. Finally, from about 1770 onwards, certain forms were developed in England which had international repercussions under the Empire in France.

The candlestick designed to hold a single candle could be transformed into a candelabrum by adding two, three or four branches to its socket. In this way it could be converted into a magnificent object, and they were generally placed in pairs at either end of a table.

The Taper-Box

A less costly lighting appliance than the wax or tallow candle was a long wick coated with a thin covering of wax and wound in a reel so that it could be easily carried. Wax tapers of this kind were also used as night-lights beside the bed. Silversmiths made boxes or lamps in which the wound taper could be kept and automatically extinguished after a certain time.

These little wick-holders or taper-boxes replaced the chamber candlestick in Italy. They were made to look like a tablet of soap and

368 Taper-box or wax jack, London, *c.* 1680. Hallmarks of a master silversmith with the initials PR. Museum of Fine Arts, Boston. (Theodora Wilbour Fund.) 61.185.

369 Taper-box, Zurich, *c.* 1720, by Hans Ulrich Körner, master silversmith 1707-40. Swiss National Museum, Zurich. LM 21208.

were often attractively decorated. Several different types of taper-box were also made in Germany. In many of these models the lighted wick was extinguished when it was nipped by the wax that had been softened by the flame.

370 Design for a taper-box, Rome, *c.* 1800, attributed to Giovacchino Belli, master silversmith 1787-1822. Cooper-Hewitt Museum, New York. 1938-88-6054.

371 Taper-box, Padua, *c.* 1740. Hallmark illegible. Private collection.

Candle-Snuffers

Scissor-shaped implements for snuffing candles go back a very long way in history. They are first mentioned in a note about the crown jewels of Queen Isabella of Bavaria in 1400. They are mentioned

372 Pair of candle-snuffers and their case, Aalborg, Denmark, *c.* 1710, by Thomas Pop. Kunstindustrimuseet, Copenhagen. 116 A-B/1958.

again in 1570 in another inventory as 'made in the German style', although it is not stated what this German style was. At that period the little box to hold the pieces of wick trimmed off the candle was heart-shaped. Later it was simply rectangular. A dish with little handles made of white silver is mentioned in Cardinal Mazarin's inventory of 1653; it is of the same type as the twenty-seven pairs of snuffers that belonged to the king in 1673. There was another, more sophisticated way of presenting snuffers: they were placed upright in a vertical stand, which looked like a tomb and so was referred to as a *tombeau*.

373 Pair of candle-snuffers in their stand with a douter, Great Britain, 1690, by John Bernard. Metropolitan Museum of Art, New York. (Gift of Irwin Untermyer, 1967.) 68.141.54 a-b-c.

374 Pair of candle-snuffers on their stand, with the arms of the Torrenté family, Leuk, Switzerland, *c.* 1720, by an unidentified craftsman. Swiss National Museum, Zurich. IN 419.

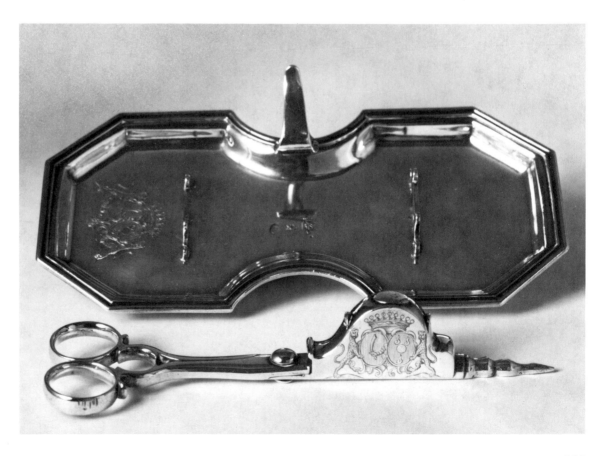

375 Pair of candle-snuffers with their stand, Lausanne, *c.* 1750, probably by Jean-François Poulet, mentioned 1745-63. Private collection.

376-377   Pair of candle-snuffers in their case, Madrid,
c. 1800, by a silversmith known as Martinez. Private
collection.

378 A lady at her toilet. A ewer and its basin, various powder and cosmetic boxes, a brush with a silver handle and a toilet-table tidy with ball feet can be seen on the table. Detail of picture attributed to Jan Gerritsz van Bronckhorst (*c.* 1603-61), Utrecht, mid-17th century. Minneapolis Institute of Arts, U.S.A. (Putnam Dana McMillan Fund.) 77.1.

379 A lady at her toilet. Print by N. Bonnart, *c.* 1690. Pierpont Morgan Library, New York,

380 A lady at her toilet. Print, *c.* 1670. Cabinet des Estampes, Bibliothèque Nationale, Paris.

Dame de Qualité à sa Toilette.
Je suis de qualité, bien-faite, jeune et belle, | Et si leur passion devenoit criminelle
Si mon ajustement pouvoit plaire aux humains | Pour moy, je m'en lave les mains.

The Toilet-Set

The French word *toilette*, which has been anglicized into 'toilet' or 'toilet-service', has been employed since the beginning of the seventeenth century for sets of articles used for care of the body, both from the point of view of hygiene and from that of physical beauty. This may point to the fact that these toilet-sets originated in France. Initially, the word simply meant the little piece of cloth in which the various toilet objects were wrapped and on which they were displayed. It was later extended to include the whole set of silver utensils used in one's toilet.

Marie de Medici and Anne of Austria are among the elegant and stylish queens who are known to have possessed attractive

259

Peint au Pastel par Ch. Coypel.   *Gravé par LeSurugue en 1745.*

La Folie pare la Décrépitude des ajustemens
de la Jeunesse.

toilet-services of the kind that were in existence from the early seventeenth century to the nineteenth. These soon became show-pieces, as striking and ostentatious as the table-ware displayed on silver sideboards. Anne of Austria was probably also the first to admit courtiers and her intimate confidants to her toilet, with the consequence that this occasion became an important daily event in the life of the court.

To judge from the many illustrations of ladies receiving fashionable guests while at their toilet, referred to earlier, this practice must have become widely accepted everywhere within a short time. Objects of an increasingly sumptuous and brilliant kind, which had clearly been created only for display, were laid out on the 'little cloth' or *toilette*. The latter lost its original meaning and was

381   A lady at her toilet. Detail of print by C. Coypel, 1745. Cabinet des Estampes, Bibliothèque Nationale, Paris.

382   Mirror and ewer with basin, part of the toilet-service of Stéphanie de Beauharnais, Grand Duchess of Baden, Paris, *c.* 1809/11, by Martin Guillaume Biennais (1764-1843). Badisches Landesmuseum, Karlsruhe.

383   Part of a toilet-set in its case, including a casket, a big powder-box, a pair of ▷ candlesticks, a chamber candlestick, bellows for powdering the hair, a number of boxes and other articles. Augsburg, *c.* 1710, by a master silversmith with the initials TB. Private collection.

384 *Le Matin*. A lady at her toilet receiving a priest for breakfast. Print by Nicolas Lancret. Cabinet des Estampes, Bibliothèque Nationale, Paris.

385 Silver-gilt toilet-set in its travelling-case. This set belonged to the estate of ▷ Duke Karl-Eugen of Wurtemberg (1737-93). Augsburg, 1755/7, by Gottlieb Satzger and Johann Georg Kloss, master silversmith 1738-66. Württembergisches Landesmuseum, Stuttgart. 1938/138-174.

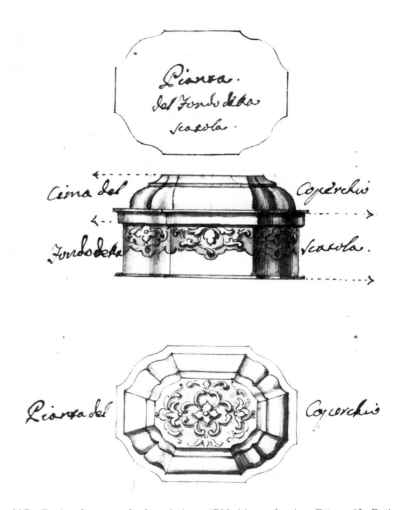

386 Cream container, Paris, 1739/40, by Claude Dargent, master silversmith 1722- c. 1780. Metropolitan Museum of Art, New York. (Bequest of Catherine D. Wentworth, 1948.) 48.187.268.

387 Design for a powder-box, Italy, c. 1720. Musée des Arts Décoratifs, Paris. CD 4284, fol. 114.

388 Sugar-box, North America, c. 1720, by John Coney (1655-1722). Museum ▷ of Fine Arts, Boston. (Bequest of Charles Hitchcock Tyler.) 32.370.

replaced by a covering of fine, intricately-woven lace, permanently laid on the toilet-table with its central mirror.

The few sets of toilet articles that have stayed together and escaped the melting-pot are all in an exceptionally good state of preservation. This shows clearly enough that these superb articles rapidly became mere showpieces. Another more modest set was used in private, while the handsome and costly one was exhibited to visitors. The toilet-service displayed by Anne of Austria was incomparably sumptuous, if one may judge simply by its case. This is studded with openwork silver-gilt flowers and foliage. It was

made in Paris, the only major centre where such cases and their contents were produced both for the court and for export.

Only four seventeenth-century toilet-sets have in fact survived. One of these, now in Edinburgh, was made in Paris in 1674 for the Duchess of Richmond and must have served as a model on which English silversmiths based their own work. In the seventeenth century toilet-sets contained no more than about a dozen different articles. The most important of them was always the mirror. This usually had a metal frame and could be placed at an angle. It generally stood at the back of the toilet-table. Often silver toilet-sets

389 Design for a toilet-casket, Paris, *c.* 1730, attributed to Jacques III Roët-tiers. Kunstbibliothek, Berlin (Staatliche Museen Preussischer Kulturbesitz). Hdz 323.

390 Silver-gilt toilet-casket, London, 1716, by James Fraillon, mentioned from ▷ 1710. Metropolitan Museum of Art, New York. (Gift of Irwin Untermyer, 1968.) 68.141.160.

contained a mirror that was not framed in silver, since only very few members of society were able to afford such a luxury.

We have already considered, in the first part of this typological survey, the next most important item in the toilet-set. This is the ewer and basin, which were almost always made of precious metal. They were in no way different from those used at table, and quite often the same ewer and basin were employed for both purposes. It is, however, interesting to note that the neck of the toilet ewer was usually not too narrow and that a favourite shape in the seventeenth century was the inverted helmet. In order to keep the water warm, ewers were often provided with a lid. In the eighteenth century ewers were only produced for toilet purposes; there was no further use for them at table because of the widespread employment of cutlery and table napkins.

The seventeenth-century toilet-service also contained a number of boxes, each with a specific purpose. There were, for example, little rectangular caskets, containing either jewels and ornaments or pots of cream and make-up. The latter were hardly different from the covered beakers that were used at meals. There were also boxes containing roots and aromatic herbs from which scents were made after soaking them in alcohol. Chamber and table candlesticks also formed an integral part of the toilet-set. Finally, there were spherical soap- and sponge-boxes, which were usually made to match, the sponge-box being fitted with a pierced lid so that the sponge could dry.

267

392

393

391 Fruit-box, Paris, 1764, by Antoine-Sébastien Durand, master silversmith 1740. Private collection.

392 Powder-box, Copenhagen, 1750, by Jonas Heinrich Jonassen. Kunstindustrimuseet, Copenhagen. A 38/1914.

393 Design for a powder-box, Germany, c. 1740. Musée des Arts Décoratifs, Paris. CD 4284, fol. 119.

394 Cream pot, part of the toilet-service of Stéphanie de Beauharnais, Grand Duchess of Baden, Paris, c. 1809/11, by Martin Guillaume Biennais (1764-1843). Badisches Landesmuseum, Karlsruhe.

The London silversmith Paul de Lamerie made a toilet-set in 1725 which included a great number of objects apart from those which could be regarded as absolutely indispensable, i.e. those more often associated with travelling-sets. The presence here of a soup-bowl or porringer, coffee-pot, milk-jug, plates and cutlery shows that by this time the toilet and the first meal of the day took place together.

It was in the eighteenth century, too, that Augsburg became the third great centre where toilet-sets were made. The ever-enterprising silversmiths of this city made a great number of interesting gadgets in addition to the traditional articles. These included trays of various kinds, glove-containers, make-up and cosmetic boxes, scent-bottles and flasks, brushes of all kinds, hand-

394

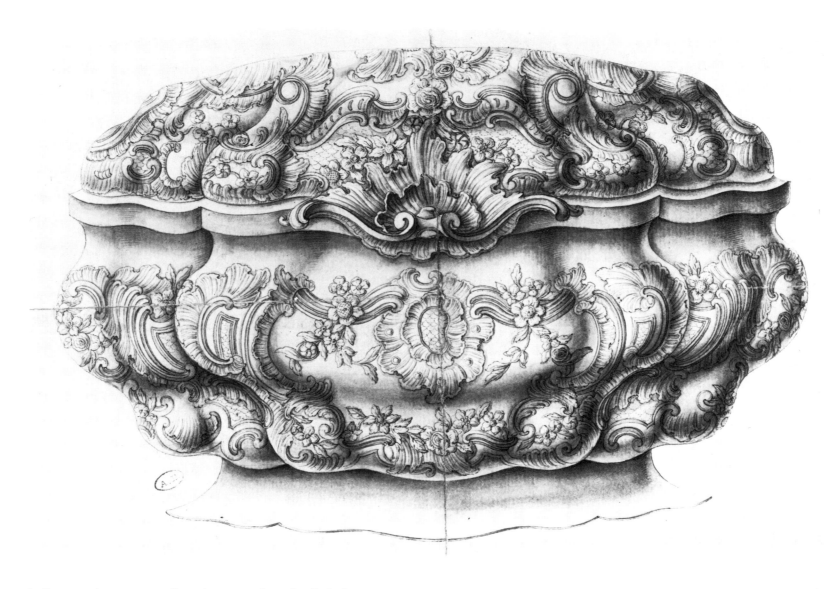

bells, cassolettes or perfume-burners, funnels, little instruments for blood-letting, boxes for pins and pin-cushions, comb-cases, vinaigrettes and eye-baths.

One toilet article closely resembles a sugar-caster and was used for sprinkling powder on one's hair or wig. Many other objects were added to toilet-services in the late eighteenth and early nineteenth centuries. The biggest of these was undoubtedly the warming-pan. This had a pierced cover to allow the heat from the glowing embers in the pan to warm the bed and a long handle so that it could be slid into the bed. Before this time such articles had hardly ever been made of silver, but the toilet-service reached a peak of perfection during the Empire period.

395 Design for a powder-box, Augsburg, *c.* 1750. Musée des Arts Décoratifs, Paris. CD 4284, fol. 78.

396　Sponge-box with coat of arms of Fernando de Susa e Silva, Paris, 1760/1. Hallmark illegible. Museu Nacional de Arte Antiga, Lisbon. Est. 39 (1).

397-398　Scent-bottle or vinaigrette, with a little receptacle for rouge at the bottom, Basle, early 18th century. This type of object seldom has hallmarks. Private collection.

399 *La Petite Singerie*. In the foreground are two silver perfume-burners. Mural painting by Christophe Huet (d. 1759). Musée Condé, Chantilly.

400 Perfume-burner, forming part of the toilet-service belonging to Stéphanie ▷ de Beauharnais, Grand Duchess of Baden, Paris, *c.* 1809/11, by Martin Guillaume Biennais (1764-1843). Badisches Landesmuseum, Karlsruhe.

273

The Inkstand and Writing-Set

As we have seen, most silver objects in wealthy households were designed for the dining-table, the silver sideboard or the toilet-table, at least before the nineteenth century. One exception was the silver inkstand or standish. Even though there has never been any impelling hygienic or practical reason for doing so, sets of writing materials have frequently been made of precious metal ever since the Middle Ages. Such sets have always included one or two ink-pots, a sand or pounce-box, a bell and a number of pens or quills, all placed on a tray.

Writing-sets have been made in every country in Europe and since the seventeenth century silver has often been used for them. Flemish sets were perhaps the first to contain a silver candlestick, not only to provide the writer with light, but also to melt sealing-wax. There is a fine specimen made by the famous craftsmen van Vianen which provides evidence of this.

Louis XIV of France possessed several silver writing-sets designed after drawings by the greatest artists of the period. The prototype of the commonest kind in the eighteenth century—not only in France, but also in England, Germany, Portugal, Spain and Italy—was created by Jean Bérain. This basic model included a tray, made in a variety of shapes and decorated in different ways, on which were placed three little vessels: the first contained the ink-pot, the second the sand-box and the third, in the middle, the hand-bell.

Many sets were made in Italy, especially in Genoa, during the eighteenth century. Those produced in Rome were in the form of cylindrical boxes, a type also found in Portugal.

Silver Furniture

Very little silver furniture has ever been made. This remarkable phenomenon was restricted to one very short period of human history and to one place—the court of the Sun King. It would, however, be wrong to overlook completely Louis XIV's silver furniture in a study devoted to domestic silverware in the modern era.

Unfortunately, nothing—or very little—has survived of these dazzling silver furnishings. The king himself conceived the idea. His painters and specialists in the decorative arts drew the designs, which were carried out in silver by the most highly skilled craftsmen working in France at the time. Silver was chosen as the

401 Writing-set, London, *c.* 1630, by an unidentified master with the initials WR. Museum of Fine Arts, Boston. (Theodora Wilbour Fund.) 1954.87.

402 Writing-set with coat of arms of Bishop Frei Luis de Silva Telles, Lisbon, ▷ 1690, by a master craftsman with the initials MDO. Museu de Évora, Portugal.

material most likely to resist the ravages of time—the king's silver furniture was to last for ever. Alas, silver also proved to be the most vulnerable of all materials. Precisely because it was so magnificent and costly, it was at once consigned to the melting-pot by the government when it needed money. Now all that remains to give us an insight into the brilliant effect achieved by the silver furnishings of the Versailles court are a few paintings illustrating royal interiors. Those responsible for staging this superb production at the palace were Charles Lebrun and the Sun King himself.

It hardly needs to be said that silver furniture was admirably suited to express the style of the period. Table-legs, for example, were copiously decorated with figures, caryatids, foliage, flowers, fruit and moulded volutes; their surfaces bore inlay work consisting

403 Design for writing-set, Rome, first quarter of 18th century. Cooper-Hewitt Museum, New York. 1938-88-8125.

404 Venetian writing-set. Detail of portrait in oils of Carlo Goldoni by ▷ Alessandro Longhi, Venice, 1757. Casa Goldoni, Venice.

of multicoloured pieces of marble or semi-precious stones. The pedestal tables or ornamental lampstands to hold sumptuous cut-glass candelabra reflected the brilliance of the candle-light. Louis XIV was particularly fond of orange-trees and the great apartments of the palace at Versailles were transformed into veritable greenhouses. The shrubs in the king's apartments were kept, not in ordinary cases but in great solid silver urns mounted on

276

405 Writing-set containing a pen-holder, two inkwells, a sand-box and a little bell, Spain, 1723, by a master with the initials AS. Private collection.

406 Writing-set. Detail from portrait of Henri-Constance de Lort de Sérignan de Valras, Bishop of Mâcon, *c.* 1763, by J.-B. Greuze (1725-1805). Musée municipal des Ursulines, Mâcon.

407 Writing-set, Zurich, early 18th century, by Hans-Ulrich Wolff, master silversmith 1701-22. Swiss National Museum, Zurich. 1417.

279

408 Writing-set. From a print by J.-M. Moreau le Jeune, 1776. Private collection.

409 Miniature writing-set, London, by John King, mentioned between 1785 ▷ and 1795. Private collection.

281

elegant stands. These ancient urns looked forward to the silver wine-coolers of a century later. There were also ewers, table-fountains, wine and wine-glass coolers and jugs, all of exceptional size, either on or beside the tables set out along the entire length of the Hall of Mirrors. The hall itself was lit by a series of silver chandeliers. The king sat on a silver throne when he received foreign visitors. It would be difficult if not impossible to describe the effect produced on foreigners by this French version of Ali Baba's cave!

Although the magnificence of Louis XIV's silver furnishings was admired by many of his contemporaries, others were deeply shocked by it. Certainly members of other courts in Germany, Scandinavia and eastern Europe wanted to imitate the luxury of the French court, but they were not able to afford it. The silversmiths of Augsburg therefore soon began to specialize in making furniture covered with very thin silver-leaf. These accurate copies were much less costly than the French originals, but they were very fragile; partly for this reason they too disappeared quickly from the scene.

Silver furniture had a very short life, but it exerted great influence on later eighteenth-century taste, especially in Germany and Italy. The fashion for silver frames for pictures and mirrors dates back to this period, when it was inaugurated by the Italian Mannerists, with their insatiable appetite for luxury. Elegant society ladies wanted silver to enclose the mirrors they used in their apartments and on their toilet-tables, as if these were altars of the Church Triumphant.

Conclusion

The great enthusiasm shown by so many amateurs and collectors for objects made of silver — a material that is noble and precious, but at the same time durable and relatively reasonably priced — has led to the appearance, in the past twenty or so years, of a great number of books on silverware, most of them lavishly illustrated. At a time when almost all works of art have been rising steadily in price, the purchase of silver objects is fully justified, both because they are intrinsically valuable and because they are so massive and substantial. A piece of china-ware, for example, can be restored by a skilful craftsman if it is broken or damaged, but its value is permanently reduced by the breakage. A silver object, on the other hand, can continue to be used without being in any way devalued; a gifted silversmith can usually repair damage perfectly and remove any trace of an accident.

Most collectors specializing in the decorative arts prefer objects that were produced in local workshops or came originally from certain internationally famous centres. Collectors of silverware are no different and they inevitably look for pieces made in such centres as Paris, London, Strasbourg, Nuremberg or Augsburg. For a long time, therefore, considerable importance was attached to the presence of hallmarks on silver articles, since these have always been regarded as proof of local manufacture or as evidence of a famous maker. At the same time, however, this emphasis on hallmarks, their presence and identification, has led to a neglect of the works' aesthetic qualities, their technical brilliance and their originality of design; it is now thought by many to have been greatly exaggerated. After all, the fact that a piece of silver is hallmarked is not an indisputable guarantee of its authenticity. So many signatures on drawings and paintings have been proved to be forgeries and even many pieces of furniture have been falsely marked. This is surely sufficient evidence of the unreliable nature of such markings.

From the very earliest times, silversmiths have been obliged by most states to hallmark their work as a guarantee, among other things, that the silver that they used was alloyed in accordance with established rules and fixed standards, so that money could be satisfactorily minted from it. In this way it was possible to avoid any possibility of fraud and to protect both the state and those who bought and used silver. An elaborate system of checks and controls was developed. It differed from town to town and from country to country and was often extremely complicated; it led to a great number of hallmarks being struck by various bodies which were responsible for guaranteeing the standard of the silver used and by the silversmiths themselves who accepted that responsibility. It is important, however, to bear in mind that the presence of a hallmark on a silver object did not necessarily correspond to the signature of the master craftsman in question. A hallmarked object might simply be a piece of silverware sold by that silversmith or only partly made by him, the other parts having been obtained from a specialist in that type of work. The master craftsmen of Nuremberg and Augsburg, for example, produced a number of very finely made pieces without hallmarks in the sixteenth and seventeenth centuries and sold them everywhere in Europe.

The same applies to charge and discharge marks. These bear witness to a tax which silversmiths tried to avoid paying by purchasing their materials at fairs and centres where they were less heavily taxed. It was even possible in certain cases to avoid all supervision by having a piece made on the model of an object that had previously been subjected to control or had belonged to a tax-exempt religious community or royal house. This explains why there are so many silver objects in existence, many of them of exceptionally high quality, which are undoubtedly authentic, despite the fact that they are not hallmarked. On the other hand, many objects have hallmarks which appear to be genuine, but only a very careful examination of their functional and aesthetic qualities will reveal where and when they originated — that is, in which centre or town, in whose workshop or at what period. Forgers have always, after all, been able to imitate and apply authentic earlier hallmarks and to strike false ones, and unfortunately these practices have often proved impossible to expose.

Since Rosenberg, Beuque and Tardy published their encyclopaedic works, many excellent collections of hallmarks have appeared containing either photographic reproductions, which have the advantage of being very exact, or line drawings, which are easily deciphered, of the many different master's marks, town marks, charge and discharge marks and guild and assay marks. The identification of these marks has been made much easier by the publication of many useful analytical tables, but this is still a long and difficult task which cannot be done without consulting a large number of reference books, many of them difficult to obtain.

Since excessive importance is attached nowadays to identifying silver objects by means of hallmarks, I have deliberately avoided this aspect of silverware, despite its obvious fascination. My aim has been to keep the scale of my study within reasonable limits. With this in mind I have followed a historical approach to the subject and have restricted it to silverware in the European tradition. To this end, I have reviewed above all the habits and characteristics of those who used these objects in their social and historical context, and considered those factors which have played a part in their creation. I hope that, in so doing, I have succeeded in describing these objects more precisely and in placing them in the historical setting in which they were originally presented and used.

Appendix

Hallmarks of Towns

where the objects illustrated in this volume were made

Aalborg

Amsterdam

Antwerp

Augsburg

Basle

Berlin

Berne

Biberach

Biel/Bienne

Birmingham

Bologna

Bordeaux

Breslau (Wrocław)

Brussels

Budapest

Burgdorf

Copenhagen		London	
Delft	Genoa		
Dijon	Göteborg		
Dresden	The Hague		
	Hamburg		
Dublin	Köping	Lyons	
Edinburgh	Lachen		
Elbing	Lausanne	Mâcon	
Frankfurt		Madrid	
Geneva	Lisbon	Malmö	

288

Mantua		Padua	St. Quentin
Moscow		Paris	Schaffhausen
Munich			Seville
			Stockholm
Naples		Parma	
		Rome	Strasbourg
Neuchâtel			
Nuremberg		St. Petersburg	
Oporto			Stuttgart

289

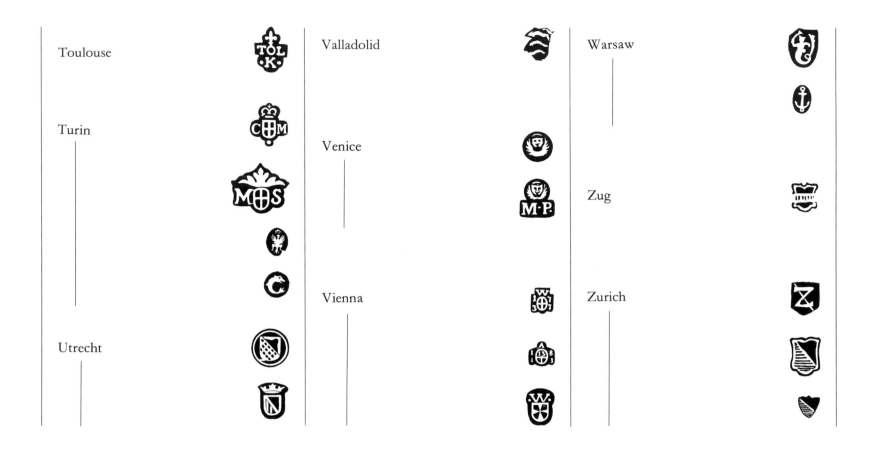

Toulouse

Turin

Utrecht

Valladolid

Venice

Vienna

Warsaw

Zug

Zurich

Bibliography

ACCASCINA, M., *I marchi delle argenterie e oreficerie siciliane*, Busto Arsizio, 1976

[Amsterdam, Rijksmuseum] *Catalogus van goud- en zilverwerken benevens zilveren, loden en bronzen plaquetten*, 2 pts., Amsterdam, 1952

ANDRÉN, E., HELLNER, B., and others, *Svenskt silversmide 1520-1850*, Stockholm, 1963

AVERY, C. L., *Early New York Silver*, New York, 1974

BAPST, G., *Etudes sur l'orfèvrerie française au 18ᵉ siècle: les Germain, orfèvres-sculpteurs du Roy*, Paris – London, 1887

BARGONI, A., 'Marchiature dell' argento in Piemonte nei secoli 17 et 18', in *Cronache economiche delle C.C.I.A.A.*, Turin, January 1967, fasc. 289, pp. 1-6

—, *Mastri orafi e argentieri in Piemonte dal XVII al XIX secolo*, Turin, 1976

BARR, E., *George Wickes 1698-1761*, London, 1980

BARTH, U., *Altes Basler Silbergerät im Hause zum 'Kirschgarten'*, Basle, 1977

—, *Zur Geschichte des Basler Goldschmiedhandwerks* (1261-1820), thesis, Basle, 1978

BENDEL, M., 'Schaffhauser Goldschmiede des XV. und XVI. Jahrhunderts', 2 pts., in *Anzeiger für schweizerische Altertumskunde*, N.S., XXXIV, fasc. 1, XXXVIII, 1936, fasc. 2

BENGTSSON, B., 'Aeltere Quellen zur Kenntnis der Goldschmiedetechnik', in *Opuscula in honorem C. Hernmarck 27.12.66*, Stockholm, 1966, pp. 11-21

BENGTSSON, B. and MUNTHE, G. L., *Silversmide. Konsthistoria och Teknik*, Stockholm, 1962

BENTLEY KOLTER, J., *Early American Silver and Its Makers*, New York, 1979

BERCKENHAGEN, E., *Die Französischen Zeichnungen der Kunstbibliothek Berlin*, Berlin, 1970

BERGAU, R., *Wentzel Jamnitzers Entwürfe zu Prachtgefässen in Silber und Gold*, Berlin, 1881

BERLINER, R. *Ornamentale Vorlage-Blätter*, 3 vols., Leipzig, 1926

BEUQUE, E., *Platine, or et argent*, Paris, 1962

BEUQUE, E., and FRAPSAUCE, M., *Dictionnaire des poinçons de maîtres-orfèvres français du XIVᵉ siècle à 1833*, Paris, 1964

BLAAUWEN, A.L. den, *Nederlands zilver*, Amsterdam, 1979

BOESEN, G., and LASSEN, E., *De danske Dronningers Guldtoilette*, Copenhagen, 1955

BOESEN, G., 'L'argenterie française dans les collections royales danoises', in *Revue du Louvre* 15, Paris, 1965, pp. 125-30

—, 'Le service de toilette de Hedvig Sofia', in *Opuscula in honorem C. Hernmarck 27.12.66*, Stockholm, 1966, pp. 22-38

—, 'Noget om drikkeskik og drikkekar i Danmarck', in *Arv og eje*, Aalborg, 1968, pp. 7-167

BOESEN, G., and BØJE, CHR. A., *Gammelt dansk sølv til bordburg*, Copenhagen, 1948

BÖHM, E., *Hans Petzolt, ein deutscher Goldschmied*, Munich, 1939

BORG, T., *Guld och Silversmeder i Finland 1373-1873*, Helsingfors, 1935

BOUILHET, H., *L'orfèvrerie française aux 18 et 19ᵉ siècle (1700-1900)*, Paris, 1908-12

BOURQUIN, W., *600 Jahre Bieler Goldschmiedegewerbe*, Biel, 1961

BRADBURY, F., *History of Old Sheffield Plate. Being an Account of the Origin, Growth, and Decay of the Industry and of the Antique Silver*, London, 1912, reprint 1968

BRAULT, S., and BOTTINEAU, Y., 'L'orfèvrerie française du 18ᵉ siècle', in *L'œil du connaisseur*, Paris, 1959

BRAULT-LERCH, S., *Les Orfèvres du Franche-Comté*, Geneva, 1976

BRUNNER, H., *Altes Tafelsilber*, Munich, 1964

BUHLER, K. C., 'The Campbell Museum Collection of Silver', in *The Connoisseur*, 173 (1970: 1), pp. 51-60

—, *American Silver 1655-1825 in the Museum of Fine Arts, Boston*, Boston, 1972

BULGARI, C.G., 'Argentieri, gemmari e orafi d'Italia', in *Notizie storiche e raccolta dei loro contrassegni con la riproduzione grafica dei punzoni individuali e dei punzoni di stato*, Rome, 1958-74, pp. 1-4

BURGESS, F.W., *Chats on Old Copper and Brass*, London, 1914

—, *Silver Pewter and Sheffield Plate*, New York, 1937

BURSCHE, S., *Tafelzier des Barock*, Munich, 1974

BYRN, FREIHERR O., *Die Hofsilberkammer und Hofkellerei zu Dresden*, Dresden, 1880

CAMÓN AZNAR, J., *La arquitectura y la orfebrerie españolas del siglo 16*, (Summa artis, 17), 3rd ed., Madrid, 1970

CANDIAGO, A., 'Un tesoro di oreficeria romana del secolo 18 a Lisbona: gli argenti di S. Rocco', in *Offprint: Estudos italianos em Portugal*, no. 24, 1965-6

CARRÉ, L., *Les Poinçons de l'orfèvrerie française du 14ᵉ siècle jusqu'au début du 19ᵉ siècle*, Paris, 1928

—, *Guide de l'amateur d'orfèvrerie française*, Paris, 1974

CARRINGTON, J. B., and HUGHES, G. R., *The Plate of the Worshipful Company of Goldsmiths*, Oxford, 1926

CASTRES, E. de, *A Collector's Guide to Tea Silver, 1670-1900*, London, 1977

CATELLO, E., and C., *Argenti Napoletani dal XVI al XIX secolo*. Preface by Bruno Molajoli, Naples, 1973

CAZENEUVE, P. de, *Du contrôle des ouvrages d'or et d'argent et des poinçons de garantie, antérieurement au 19 brumaire an VI*, Algiers, 1895

CEDERSTRÖM, R., *De svenska riksregalierna och kungliga värdighet-stecknen*, Stockholm, 1942

CITROËN, K. A., *Amsterdam Silversmiths and their Marks*, Amsterdam, 1975

COUTO, J., and GONÇALVES, A., *A ourivesaria em Portugal*, Lisbon, 1960

DAUTERMAN, C. C., 'English Silver in an American Company Museum', in *The Connoisseur*, 159, 1964/5, pp. 206-11

DAVILIER, C., *Recherches sur l'orfèvrerie en Espagne*, Paris, 1879

DAVIS, F., *French Silver 1450-1825*, London, 1970

DENNIS, F., *Three Centuries of French Domestic Silver*, New York, 1960

DICK, E., 'Un Orfèvre lausannois, Pierre-Henry Dautun', in *Revue historique vaudoise*, 59, 1951

DIDEROT, D., and ALEMBERT, J., *Le Rond d'Encyclopédie ou Dictionnaire raisonné des sciences, des arts et des métiers*. 3rd ed., Livorno, 1770-81

[Dortmund, Museum für Kunst und Kulturgeschichte] *Gold und Silber. Beschreibendes und kritisches Verzeichnis der Goldschmiede-arbeiten des 12.-18. Jahrhunderts*, Dortmund, 1965

[—] *Schloss Cappenberg. Silberarbeiten beschrieben von Hans Appuhn*, Dortmund, 1973

DURRER, R., 'Goldschmiedearbeiten aus dem Atelier Bossard', in *Wegleitungen des Kunstgewerbemuseums Zürich*, 43, 1922

DÜRST, H., 'Der Bremgarter Bürgerschatz', in *Bremgarter Neujahrs-blätter*, 1962

DUYVENE, TH. M., and GANS, M. H., *Geschiedenis van het nederlanse zilver*, Amsterdam, 1958

ESTERAS MARTIN, C., *Orfebreria de Teruel y su provincia, siglos 13 al 20*, Teruel, 1980

EVANS, J., *Huguenot Goldsmiths in England and Ireland*, London, 1933

FILIMONOV, G., *Opis moskovskoy Oruzheynoy palati*, 2 vols., Moscow, 1884-5

FILLITZ, H., and NEUMANN, E., 'Barock in Böhmen', in *Das Kunstgewerbe*, ed. by Karl M. Swoboda, 1964, pp. 275-345

FINLAY, I., *Scottish Gold and Silver Work*, London, 1956

FORNARI, S., *Gli argenti romani*, Rome, 1968

FOZ, Triatão Guedes de Queiroz Correia Castello-Branco, Marquês da, *A baixela Germain da antiga côrte portuguesa*, Lisbon, 1926

FRANKENBURGER, M., *Die Alt-Münchner Goldschmiede und ihre Kunst*, Munich, 1912

—, *Die Silberkammer der Münchner Residenz*, Munich, 1923

FREDERIKS, J. W., *Dutch Silver*, 4 vols., The Hague, 1952-61
   1. Embossed Plaquettes, Tazze and Dishes from the Renaissance until the End of the 18th Century
   2. Wrought Plate of North and South Holland from the Renaissance until the End of the 18th Century
   3. Wrought Plate of the Central, Northern and Southern Provinces from the Renaissance until the End of the 18th Century
   4. Embossed Ecclesiastical and Secular Plate from the Renaissance until the End of the 18th Century

FRITZ, J. M., 'Gestochene Bilder. Gravierungen auf deutschen Goldschmiedearbeiten der Spätgotik', in *Beihefte der Bonner Jahrbücher*, vol. 20, Cologne, 1966

FRITZ, R., *Sammlung August Neresheimer*, Hamburg-Altona, 1974

FROST, T. W., *Old Sheffield Plate*, Indianapolis, 1977

GASK, N., 'Old Silver Spoons of England', in *A Guide for Collectors*, London, 1926

GERMAIN, P., *Eléments d'orfèvrerie divisés en deux parties de cinquante feuilles chacune*, Paris, 1748

[GILLIERS] *Le Cannameliste Français, Ou Nouvelle Instruction Pour Ceux Qui Désirent d'Apprendre L'Office... Par le Sieur Gilliers, Chef d'Office, et Distillateur de Sa Majesté le Roi de Pologne, Duc de Lorraine et de Bar*, Nancy, 1751

GODEFROY, G., *Les Orfèvres de Lyon (1306-1791) et de Trévoux (1700-1786), Répertoire biographique. Poinçons. Œuvres*, Preface by P. Verlet, Paris, 1965

GRANDJEAN, S., 'L'Orfèvrerie du 19e siècle', in *L'œil du connaisseur*, Paris, 1962

Les Grands Orfèvres de Louis XIII à Charles X. Preface by Jacques Helft. Introduction by Jean Baelon. Texts presented by Yves Bottineau and Olivier Lefuel. (Collection 'Connaissance des Arts'. Series 'Grands artisans d'autrefois'.) Paris, 1965

GRIMWADE, A. G., 'Royal Toilet Services in Scandinavia', in *The Connoisseur*, 137 (1956: 1), pp. 175-8

—, *Rococo Silver 1727-1765* (Faber Monographs on Silver), London, 1974

—, *London Goldsmiths 1695-1837: Their Marks and Lives*, London, 1976

GRUBER, A., *Kostbares Essbesteck des 16. bis 18. Jahrhunderts*, Aus dem Schweizerischen Landesmuseum, 39, Berne, 1976

—, *Weltliches Silber. Katalog der Sammlung des Schweizerischen Landesmuseums Zürich*, Zurich, 1977

—, 'Le double-hanap de Louis Pfyffer d'Altishofen, une pièce d'orfèvrerie parisienne de l'Ecole de Fontainebleau', in *Bulletin de la Société d'Histoire de l'Art Français*, 1978, pp. 23-36

—, 'L'Orfèvrerie civile en Suisse romande', in *Trésors de l'Artisanat en Suisse romande*, Lausanne, 1979, pp. 110-27

GUTH, P., 'Le bestiaire fabuleux des orfèvres de la Renaissance allemande', in *Connaissance des Arts*, May 1954, pp. 20-5

GUTKIND, C. S., *Das Buch der Tafelfreuden*, Leipzig, 1929

GYSIN, F., *Schweizerisches Gebrauchssilber.* Aus dem Schweizerischen Landesmuseum, 3, Berne, 1954

HÄBERLE, A., *Die Goldschmiede zu Ulm*, Ulm, 1934

HACKENBROCH, Y., *English and Other Silver in the Irwin Untermyer Collection*, New York, 1963, rev. ed. New York, 1969

—, *Highlights of Silver in the Irwin Untermyer Collection of English and Continental Decorative Arts*, New York, 1977

HAUG, H., 'Strasbourg pendant cinq siècles, une des capitales de l'orfèvrerie européenne', in *Connaissance des Arts*, 1964, No. 151, pp. 102-11

HAVARD, H., *Dictionnaire de l'ameublement et de la décoration depuis le 13e siècle jusqu'à nos jours*, 4 vols., Paris, 1887-90

—, *Histoire de l'orfèvrerie française*, Paris, 1896

HAYWARD, J. F., *English Cutlery*, London, 1957

—, 'Silver Furniture', 1-4, in *Apollo*, 65 (1958: 1), pp. 71-4, 124-7, 153-7, 220-3

—, 'A Rock-Crystal Bowl from the Treasury of Henry VIII', in *The Burlington Magazine*, 100 (1958), pp. 120, 122-5

—, *Huguenot Silver in England, 1688-1727* (Faber Monographs on Silver, 1), London, 1959

—, 'The Mannerist Goldsmiths: 1. Italian Sources. And some Drawings and Designs', in *The Connoisseur*, 149 (1962: 1), pp. 156-65

—, 'The Mannerist Goldsmiths: 2. France and the School of Fontainebleau', in *The Connoisseur*, 152 (1963: 1), pp. 240-5; 153 (1963: 2), pp. 11-15

—, 'The Mannerist Goldsmiths: 3. Antwerp', in *The Connoisseur*, 156 (1964: 2), pp. 92-6, 164-70, 250-4; 158 (1965: 1), pp. 144-9

—, 'The Mannerist Goldsmiths: 4. England', in *The Connoisseur*, 159 (1965: 2), pp. 80-4; 162 (1966: 2) pp. 90-5; 164 (1967: 1), pp. 19-25

—, 'The Mannerist Goldsmiths: 5. Germany', in *The Connoisseur*, 164 (1967: 1), pp. 78-84, 148-54, 216-22; 165 (1967: 2), pp. 162-7; 168 (1968: 2), pp. 15-19, 161-6; 175 (1970: 3), pp. 22-30

—, *The Courtauld Silver*, London – New York, 1975

—, *Virtuoso Goldsmiths and the Triumph of Mannerism 1570-1620*, London, 1976

HEITMANN, B., *Die deutschen sogenannten Reise-Service und die Toiletten-Garnituren von 1680 bis zum Ende des Rokoko und ihre kulturgeschichtliche Bedeutung*, thesis, Hamburg, 1979

HELFT, J., 'Pour s'y connaître mieux en tasses à vin', in *Connaissance des Arts*, June 1962, pp. 60-5

—, *Le Poinçon des provinces françaises*, Paris, 1968

—, *Nouveaux poinçons*, Paris, 1980

HEPPE, K. B. *Barocke Pracht*, Unna, 1978

—, *Gold und Silber aus dem Münsterland, von der Renaissance bis zum Klassizismus*, Unna, 1981

HERNMARCK, C., *The Art of the European Silversmith, 1430-1830*, London – New York, 1977

—, 'Claude Ballin et quelques dessins de pièces d'argenterie du Musée national de Stockholm', in *Gazette des beaux-arts*, 6: 41 (1953: 1), pp. 103-18

—, 'Hamburg und der schwedische Hof während des 17. Jahrhunderts', in *Festschrift für Erich Meyer zum 60. Geburtstag 29. Okt. 1957*, Hamburg, 1959, pp. 273-86

HEUSER, H. J., *Oberrheinische Goldschmiedekunst im Hochmittelalter*, Berlin, 1974

HINTZE, E., *Schlesische Goldschmiede*, Osnabrück, 1979

HONOUR, H., *Goldsmiths and Silversmiths*, London, 1971

HOUART, V., *L'Argenterie miniature*, Fribourg, 1981

HÜSELER, K., 'Hamburger Silber 1600-1800', in *Wohnkunst und Hausrat, einst und jetzt*, 18, Darmstadt, 1955

JACKSON, C. J., *An Illustrated History of English Plate, Ecclesiastical and Secular, in Which the Development of Form and Decoration in the Silver and Gold Work of the British Isles from the Earliest Known Examples to the Latest of the Georgian Period is Delineated and Described*, 2 vols., London, 1911

—, *English Goldsmiths and their Marks. A History of the Goldsmiths and Plate-Workers of England, Scotland and Ireland*, 2nd rev. and enl. ed., London, 1921

JANSEN, B., *Nederlands zilver 1815-1960*, The Hague, 1960

JESSEN, P., *Der Ornamentstich. Geschichte der Vorlagen des Kunsthandwerks seit dem Mittelalter*, Berlin, 1920

—, *Meister des Ornamentstichs. Eine Auswahl aus vier Jahrhunderten*, Berlin, 1921-4

JOHNSON, A. M., *Hispanic Silverwork* (with a catalogue of silverwork in the collection of the Hispanic Society of America), New York, 1944

JONES, E. A., *The Gold and Silver of Windsor Castle*, Letchworth, 1911

JOURDAN-BARRY, R., *Les Orfèvres de la généralité d'Aix-en-Provence du XIVᵉ siècle au début du XIXᵉ siècle*, Paris, 1974

KAISER, J., *Die Zuger Goldschmiedekunst bis 1830*, thesis, University of Zurich, Zug, 1927

[Kassel, Königliche Sammlungen] *Ältere Silberarbeiten in den Königlichen Sammlungen zu Cassel*. Mit urkundlichen Nachrichten und einem Anhang: Der Hessen-Casselsche Silberschatz zu Anfang des 17. Jahrhunderts und seine späteren Schicksale. Ed. by C. Alhard von Drach. Marburg in Hessen, 1888

KOECHLIN, R., 'L'écuelle de Thomas Germain', in *Bulletin des musées de France*, 1908: 1, pp. 4-5

KOHLHAUSSEN, H., *Nürnberger Goldschmiedekunst des Mittelalters und der Dürerzeit 1240-1540*, Jahresgabe des Deutschen Vereins für Kunstwissenschaft 1967, Berlin, 1968

KOSZEGHY, E., *Merkzeichen der Goldschmiede Ungarns*, Budapest, 1936

KRIS, E., *Goldschmiedearbeiten des Mittelalters, der Renaissance und des Barock*, pt. 1. *Arbeiten in Gold und Silber* (Publikationen aus den Kunsthistorischen Sammlungen in Wien, vol. 5), Vienna, 1932

KROHN-HANSEN, T., *Trondhjems gullsmedkunst 1550-1850*, Oslo, 1963

KROHN-HANSEN, T., and KLOSTER, R., *Bergens gullsmedkunst fra laugstiden*, 2 vols., Bergen, 1957

LASSEN, E., *Ske, kniv og gaffel*, Copenhagen, 1960

—, *Dansk sølv*, Copenhagen, 1975

LASTYRIE, F. de, *Histoire de l'orfèvrerie*, Paris, 1875

LECHNER, A., 'Georg Adam Rebfues (1784-1858)', in *Blätter für bernische Geschichte, Kunst- und Altertumskunde* 4, 1908

LESSING, J., *Lechner Gold und Silber*, Handbücher der Königl. Museen zu Berlin, Berlin, 1892

LEVALLET-HAUG, G., 'Gold and Silverware at Strasbourg', in *Apollo*, N.S., 94 (1971: 2), pp. 140-4

LEVER, CH., *Goldsmiths and Silversmiths of England*, London, 1975

LIGHTBROWN, R. W., 'Christian van Vianen at the Court of Charles I', in *Apollo*, 87 (1968: 1), pp. 426-39

—, *French Silver in the Victoria and Albert Museum*, Catalogue, London, 1978

LINK, E. M., *Ullstein Silberbuch. Eine Kunst- und Kulturgeschichte des Silbers*, Frankfurt – Vienna, 1968

LIPINSKY, A., *Oreficeria e argenteria in Europa dal 16. al 19. secolo*, Novara, 1965

[Lisbon, Museu Nacional de Arte Antiga] *Roteiro da ourivesaria*, Lisbon, 1959

LÖSEL, E. M. 'Das Zürcher Goldschmiede-Handwerk im 16. und 17. Jahrhundert', in *Mitteilungen der Antiquarischen Gesellschaft in Zürich*, 46, 1975, fasc. 3

LUTHMER, F., *Gold und Silber: Handbuch der Edelschmiedekunst*, Leipzig, 1888

LUTTEMANN, H., *Serebro Shvetsii*, Moscow, 1978

McLEAN WARD, B., and WARD, G. W. R., *Silver in American Life*, Boston, 1979

MANTZ, P., 'Recherches sur l'histoire de l'orfèvrerie française', 1-5, in *Gazette des beaux-arts*, 9 (1861: 1), pp. 15-41, 82-100; 10 (1861: 2), pp. 14-28, 129-57; 11 (1861: 3), pp. 110-34, 250-61, 349-61; 14 (1863: 1), pp. 176-87, 238-54, 410-29, 534-50

MARIACHER, G., *Argenti italiani*, Milan, 1965

MARKOWA, G. A., *Deutsche Silberkunst des XVI.-XVIII. Jahrhunderts*, Moscow, 1975

MARQUET de VASSELOT, J. J., 'A propos de l'écuelle de Th. Germain', in *Bulletin des musées de France*, 1908: 2, p. 21

—, *Bibliographie de l'orfèvrerie et de l'émaillerie françaises*, Paris, 1925

MATTHEY, CH.-H., *L'orfèvrerie artistique dans le pays de Neuchâtel aux XVIIᵉ et XVIIIᵉ siècle*, Neuchâtel, 1980

MEAL, A., *The London Goldsmiths 1200-1800*, Cambridge, 1935

MEINZ, M. *Schönes Silber. Keysers Handbuch für Sammler und Liebhaber*, Munich, 1964

MOLLWO, M., *Beiträge zur Geschichte der Berner Goldschmiedekunst*, Berne, 1948

MONTAIGNE, M. de, *Journal du voyage de Michel de Montaigne en Italie par la Suisse et l'Allemagne, en 1580 et 1581*, Rome, 1774

MORASSI, A., *Antica oreficeria italiana*, Milan, 1936

MORAZZONI, G., *Argenterie Genovesi*, Milan, 1951

[Munich, Schatzkammer der Residenz] *Katalog*, 3rd ed. by H. Brunner, Munich

MUTSCHELKNAUSS, E., *Die Entwicklung des Nürnberger Goldschmiedehandwerks von seinen ersten Anfängen an bis zur Einführung der Gewerbefreiheit im Jahre 1869*, Leipzig

NEUWIRTH, W., *Lexikon Wiener Gold- und Silberschmiede und ihre Punzen, 1867-1922*, Vienna, 1976

NOCK, H., *Le Poinçon de Paris. Répertoire des maîtres-orfèvres de la juridiction de Paris depuis le Moyen Age jusqu'à la fin du XVIIIᵉ siècle*, 5 vols., Paris, 1926-31

NOCK, H., ALFASSA, P., and GUÉRIN, J., *Orfèvrerie civile française du 16ᵉ au début du 19ᵉ siècle*, 2 vols., Paris, 1927

OLRIK, J., *Danske Sølvarbejder fra Renaissance til vore Dage*, Copenhagen, 1915

OMAN, C., *English Domestic Silver*, London, 1934

—, *The Wellington Plate: Portuguese Service* (Victoria and Albert Museum Monographs, 4), London, 1954

—, *The English Silver in the Kremlin 1557-1663*, London, 1961

—, *Medieval Silver Nefs* (Victoria and Albert Museum Monographs, 15), London, 1963

—, *English Silversmiths' Work*, London, 1965

—, *The Golden Age of Hispanic Silver, 1400-1665*, London, 1968

—, *Caroline Silver, 1625-1688*, London, 1970

ORTIZ JUAREZ, D., *Punzones de platería cordobesa*, Cordoba, 1980

[Paris, Musée du Louvre and Musée de Cluny] Y. Bottineau, *Catalogue de l'orfèvrerie du 17ᵉ, du 18ᵉ et du 19ᵉ siècle*, Paris, 1958

PENZER, N. M., *Paul Storr: The Last of the Goldsmiths*. With a foreword by Charles Oman. London, 1954

—, 'The Great Wine-coolers', 2 pts., in *Apollo*, 66 (1957: 2), pp. 3-7, 29-36

PHILLIPS, P. A. S., *Paul de Lamerie, Citizen and Goldsmith of London. A Study of his Life and Work A.D. 1688-1751*, London, 1935

PROCACCHI, G., *Trincier oder Vorlege Buch... nach Italienischer und vornehmlich Romanischer Art...*, Leipzig, 1624

RAMSEY, L. G. G. (ed.), 'Antique English Silver and Plate', in *The Connoisseur New Guide*, London, 1962

RATHKE-KÖHL, S., *Geschichte des Augsburger Goldschmiedegewerbes vom Ende des 17. bis zum Ende des 18. Jahrhunderts*. (Schwäbische Geschichtsquellen und Forschungen, 6), Augsburg, 1964

—, *Augsburger Silbergeräte des Spätbarock und Geschichte des Augsburger Goldschmiedegewerbes vom Ende des 17. bis zum Ende des 18. Jahrhunderts*, thesis, Hamburg, 1964

RIBERA, A. L., and SCHENONE, H. H., *Platería Sudamericana de los siglos XVII-XX*, Munich, 1981

RICHTER, E. L., *Silber: Imitation — Kopie, Fälschung — Verfälschung*, Munich, 1982

RIDGWAY, M. H., *Chester Goldsmiths from Early Times to 1726*, Altrincham, 1968

RITTMEYER, D. F., 'Rapperswiler Goldschmiedekunst', in *Mitteilungen der Antiquarischen Gesellschaft in Zürich*, 34, 1949, fasc. 3

—, 'Hans Jakob Läublin, Goldschmied', in *Schaffhauser Biographien, 18./19. Jahrhundert*, Thaingen, 1956

—, 'Rapperswiler Silberarbeiten im Glarnerland', in *Heimatkunde vom Linthgebiet*, supplement to *St. Galler Volksblatt*, 30th year, Nos. 3-4, Uznach, 1958

—, 'Die alten Winterthurer Goldschmiede', in *Mitteilungen der Antiquarischen Gesellschaft in Zürich*, 42, 1962, fasc. 1

RITTMEYER, D. F. and STAFFELBACH, G., *Hans Peter Staffelbach. Goldschmied in Sursee 1657-1736*, Lucerne, 1936

ROHR, J. B. von, *Einleitung in die Ceremonial-Wissenschaft der grossen Herren*, Berlin, 1729

ROOSEN-RUNGE, M., née Mollwo, 'Beiträge zur Geschichte der Berner Goldschmiedekunst', in *Jahrbuch des Bernischen Historischen Museums in Bern*, XXVII, 1948; XXIX, 1950

—, 'Die Goldschmiede der Stadt Bern. Aufträge, Arbeiten und Merkzeichen', in *Jahrbuch des Bernischen Historischen Museums in Bern*, XXX, 1951

ROSENBERG, M., 'Die drei sogenannten Jamnitzer Becher', in *Kunst und Gewerbe*, 1885, pp. 298-305

—, *Studien über Goldschmiedekunst in der Sammlung Figdor, Wien*, Vienna, 1911

—, *Jamnitzer: alle erhaltenen Goldschmiedearbeiten, verlorene Werke, Handzeichnungen*, Frankfurt, 1920

—, *Der Goldschmiede Merkzeichen*, 3rd enl. and ill. ed., 4 vols., Frankfurt-Berlin, 1922-8

ROSSI, F., *Capolavori di oreficeria italiana*, Milan, 1956

ROWE, R., *Adam Silver 1765-1795*, London, 1965

RUIZ ALCON, T., 'Der Schatz des Grand Dauphin: Prado, Madrid', in *Schatzkammern Europas*, Munich, 1968, pp. 29-36

Russian Silver Ware of the XVIIth—the Beginning of the XXth Century in the State Hermitage Collection, Leningrad, 1977

SANTOS, R. dos, *Catálogo das Jóias e Pratas da Coroa, Palacio Nacional da Ajuda*, Lisbon, 1954

SANTOS, R. dos, and QUILHÓ, I., *Ourivesaria portuguesa nas colecçoes particulares*, 2 vols., Lisbon, 1959-60

SCHEFFLER, W., *Die Goldschmiede Niedersachsens*, Berlin, 1965

—, *Berliner Goldschmiede: Daten, Werke, Zeichen*, Berlin, 1968

—, *Goldschmiede Rheinland-Westfalens*, Berlin-New York, 1973

—, *Goldschmiede Hessens*, Berlin – New York, 1976

—, *Goldschmiede Mittel- und Nordostdeutschlands: von Wernigerode bis Lauenburg in Pommern*, Berlin – New York, 1980

SCHERER, P. (ed.), *Das Gmünder Schmuckhandwerk bis zum Beginn des XIX. Jahrhunderts*, Schwäbisch-Gmünd, 1971

SCHIEDLAUSKY, G., *Essen und Trinken. Tafelsitten bis zum Ausgang des Mittelalters*, Munich, 1959

—, *Tee, Kaffee, Schokolade*, Munich, 1961

SCHOLZ, R., *Goldschmiedearbeiten*, Hamburg, 1974

SCHOUBYE, S., *Das Goldschmiedehandwerk in Schleswig-Holstein*, Heide, 1967

SCHRIJVER, E., 'Europe's Earliest Silver Tea-Kettle', in *The Connoisseur*, 166 (1967: 3), pp. 81-4

SELING, H., 'Silber', in *Keysers Kunst- und Antiquitätenbuch*, vol. 1, Munich, 1957

—, *Die Kunst der Augsburger Goldschmiede 1529-1868*, 3 vols., Munich, 1980

SNODIN, M., *English Silver Spoons*, London, 1974

SOLODKOFF, A. v., *Russian Gold and Silver*, London – New York, 1981

Les Soupers de la Cour, ou l'Art de travailler toutes sortes d'alimens. Paris, 1755

STEINGRÄBER, E., *Der Goldschmied. Vom alten Handwerk der Gold- und Silberarbeiter*, Munich, 1966

—, (ed.), *Schatzkammer Europas*, Munich, 1968

[Stockholm, Nationalmuseum] *Mästerverk i Nationalmuseum. Konsthantverk.* Stockholm, 1954

Svenskt silversmide, 1520-1850. Stockholm, 1940-63

1. KÄLLSTRÖM, O., and HERNMARCK, C., *Renässans och Barock,* 1520-1700, 1940-1

2. HERNMARCK, C., STAVENOW, A., and MUNTHE, G., *Senbarock, Fredrik I: s stil och rokoko, 1700-1780*, 1942-3

3. HERNMARCK, C., ANDRÉN, E., and BENGTSSON, B., *Gustaviansk stil, Empire och Romantik. Aeldre guldsmedsteknik.* (English summary by C. Hernmarck: *A Survey of the Development of the Goldsmiths' and Silversmiths' Crafts in Sweden 1520-1850*), 1944-5

4. ANDRÉN, E., HELLNER, B., HERNMARCK, C., and HOLM-QUIST, K., *Guld- och silverstämplar*, 1962-3
Svenskt silversmide 1320-1850, 3 vols., Stockholm, 1940-1 (G. Berg, C. Hernmarck, O. Källström, A. Lindblom, G. Munthe, G. Silfverstolpe, A. Stavenow, S. Wallin, E. Wettergren)

TARDY, *Poinçons français pour l'argent de 1798 à nos jours*, Paris, 1962

TAYLOR, G., *Silver*, Harmondsworth, 1956, 2nd ed. Baltimore, 1963

—, *Art in Silver and Gold*, London, 1964

—, *Continental Gold and Silver*, London, 1967

Nicodème Tessin le jeune et Daniel Cronström: Correspondance (extraits), Les Relations artistiques entre la France et la Suède 1693-1718, (published by R.-A. Weigert and C. Hernmarck), (Nationalmusei skriftserie, 10), Stockholm, 1964

THUILE, J., *Histoire de l'orfèvrerie du Languedoc. Généralités de Montpellier et de Toulouse. Répertoire des orfèvres depuis le Moyen Age jusqu'au début du 19e siècle*, 3 vols., Paris, 1964-9

UGGLAS, C. R. af, *Senmedeltida profant silversmide i Sverige* (with German summary), Stockholm, 1942

VANWITTENBERGH, J., *Orfèvrerie au poinçon de Bruxelles*, Brussels, 1979

VERLET-RÉAUBOURG, N., *Les orfèvres du ressort de la Monnaie de Bourges*, Geneva, 1977

VERLET, P., *Le style Louis XIV*, Paris, 1945

—, 'Nouvelle acquisition du Département des objets d'art du Musée du Louvre: 1. Nécessaire de la reine Marie Leczinska', in *Revue des arts*, 6 (1956), pp. 37-40

—, 'La vaisselle d'or de Louis XV', in *Revue des arts*, 6 (1956), pp. 99-104

—, 'Louis XV et les grands services d'orfèvrerie parisienne de son temps', in *Panthéon*, 1977, pp. 131-51

WEIGERT, R. A., 'Recherches sur quelques dessins de la vaisselle du Grand Roi', in *Revue de l'histoire de Versailles et de Seine-et-Oise*, Versailles, Nov.-Dec. 1931

WILD, G., 'English and Continental Silver in the Godman Collection', in *Apollo*, 87 (1968: 1), pp. 266-73

[Williamstown, Mass., Sterling and Francine Clark Art Institute] *Paul de Lamerie*, 1953. *Old English Silver Coffee Pots and Salvers*, 1958. *Old Silver Teapots*, 1960. *Old Silver Bowls and Dishes*, 1964.

Old Silver Dining Accessories, 1965

WITTMANN, O., 'A Great Lady's Nécessaire de Voyage' in *Apollo*, 94 (1971: 2), pp. 145-9

WOLLIN, N. G., *Aeggkoppar, äggställare och äggställ* (Summary: Egg-cups, double egg-cups, egg-stands), Stockholm, 1962

WYLER, S. B., *The Book of Old Silver: English–American–Foreign. With all Available Hallmarks including Sheffield Plate Marks*, New York, 1937, 1965

Exhibitions

1929 Paris, Musée des Arts Décoratifs. *Exposition d'orfèvrerie civile française de la Révolution à nos jours*

1934 Lisbon, Museu Nacional de Arte Antiga. *Catálogo da exposiçao de obras de arte francesas existentes em Portugal. 1. Ourivesaria do século 18.* Introduction: Figueiredo, José de (also in French, printed separately)

1934 Stockholm, Nationalmuseum. *Svenskt Silver 1680-1800*

1949 Schloss Jegenstorf near Berne. *Altes Berner Silber*. Illustrated exhibition catalogue

1951 Basle, Kunsthalle. *Altes Silber aus Basler Privatbesitz*

1952 Utrecht, Centraal Museum. *Utrechts zilver*. Catalogue with introduction by Houtzager, E.

1953 Copenhagen, det danske Kunstindustriemuseum. *Dansk Sølv 1550-1950*

1955 Lisbon, Fundaçao Ricardo Espirito Santo Silva. *Exposiçao de ourivesaria portuguesa e francesa*

1959 Milan, Museo Poldi Pezzoli. *Argenti italiani dal 16. al 18. secolo*

1960 Paris, Musée des Arts Décoratifs

1963 Turin, Palazzo Madama, Palazzo Reale, Palazzina di Stupigni. *Mostra del Barocco Piemontese* (Bargoni, Augusto, *Argenti III*, pp. 1-32)

1964 Paris, chez Jacques Kugel, 7, rue de la Paix. *Le siècle d'or de l'orfèvrerie de Strasbourg*. (Introduction and biographical notes: Haug, Hans; description of objects: Fischer, Jacques)

1966 Hamburg, Altonaer Museum. *Altes Tafelgerät. Sammlung Udo und Mania Bey*

1966 Schloss Jegenstorf near Berne. *Schweizer Tafelsilber 1650-1850*. Illustrated exhibition catalogue

1968 Augsburg, Rathaus and Holbeinhaus. *Augsburger Barock*. (Müller, Hannelore, *Augsburger Goldschmiedekunst 1620-1720* and catalogue, pp. 279-387)

1970 Seville, Museo di Bellas Artes. *Orfebreria Sevillana de los siglos XIV al XVII*

1971 Berlin. Pechstein, K., *Goldschmiedewerke der Renaissance*

1975 Bonn. *Rheinische Goldschmiedekunst der Renaissance und Barockzeit*

1976 Washington. Hughes, G., *Treasures of London*

1977 Baltimore etc. Dautermann, C. C., *The Folger's Coffee Collection of Antique English Silver Coffee Pots and Accessories*

1977 Düsseldorf. Heppe, K. B., *Vierhundert Jahre Gold- und Silberschmiedekunst in Düsseldorf*

1979 London, Goldsmiths' Hall. Schroder, T., *The Schroder Collection*

1980 Cologne, Kunstgewerbemuseum der Stadt. Heuser, H. J., Klesse, B., and Schümann, C. W., *Ein rheinischer Silberschatz: Schmuck und Gerät aus Privatbesitz*

1980 Cologne. Schäfke, W., *Goldschmiedearbeiten des Historismus in Köln*

1981 Dunkirk. Messiant, G., and Pfister, Ch., *L'Orfèvrerie en Flandre*

Index

Photo Credits

The publishers wish to express their gratitude to the museums and private collectors who kindly made available the objects illustrated as follows, and also to the photographers.

This list has been compiled by Inès Claraz from information supplied by the author, but unfortunately some photographs could not be identified.

Alborg, Historiske Museum   249
Altshausen (Federal Republic of Germany)   144 (Elmar Hugger)
Amsterdam, Rijksmuseum   65, 98, 171, 310, 342
— Stedelijk Museum   220
Basle, Archiv der Hausgenossenzunft   102
— Maurice Babey   130
— Colour photo Hinz   10
Baltimore, Walters Art Gallery   35, 38, 66
Belfast, Ulster Museum   319
Berlin (West), Bildarchiv Preussischer Kulturbesitz   4, 71, 106, 124, 175, 193, 258, 259, 266, 333 (Hans-Joachim Bartsch), 389
Bologna, Biblioteca Comunale dell'Archiginnasio   5
Boston, Museum of Fine Arts   75, 76, 86, 94-6, 104, 109, 118, 153, 156, 178, 201-5, 207, 214, 217, 219, 250, 314, 321, 323, 328, 338, 339, 366, 368, 388, 401
Brussels, Bibliothèque Royale Albert Ier   2, 23
Caen, Musée des Beaux-Arts   256
Chantilly, Musée Condé   399 (Lauros-Giraudon)
Chatsworth (Derbyshire), Trustees of the Chatsworth Settlement   88, 191
Compiègne, Musée National du Château   32 (Lauros-Giraudon)
Copenhagen, Kunstindustrimuseet   100, 115, 272, 345, 372 (Ole Woldbye); 392

Évora (Portugal), Museu de   402
Florence, Archivi Alinari   1
Fribourg (Leo Hilber)   34, 36, 37, 39, 40, 42, 44, 45, 49, 50, 52, 54, 59, 61, 64, 78, 87, 90-3, 99, 101, 105, 110, 113, 122, 125-7, 131, 137, 141-3, 149, 152, 157-9, 165-7, 173, 180, 182, 198, 199, 210, 211, 223-5, 230, 231, 235, 236, 251, 253, 263, 267, 273-5, 277, 280-2, 284-6, 294, 295, 297, 301, 304-8, 315, 318, 331, 334, 340, 343, 355, 356, 371, 376, 377, 397, 398, 405, 410
Geneva, Christie's   48, 79, 188, 265, 383
Göteborg, Röhsska Konstslöjdmuseet   111, 138
Karlsruhe, Badisches Landesmuseum   282, 394, 400
Lausanne   136 (Jacques Saxod)
Lisbon, Fundação Ricardo Espirito Santo Silva   140, 218, 276
— Museu Nacional de Arte Antiga   83, 169, 213, 396
London, British Library   291
—/ Norwich, Colman Collection of Silver Mustard Pots   246-8
— Cooper Bridgeman Library   28
— Lord Chamberlain's Office   33
— National Gallery   63
— Sotheby Parke Bernet & Co.   31
— Victoria and Albert Museum   77, 139, 195, 216
— Wellington Museum   29, 30
Mâcon, Musée Municipal des Ursulines   406
Madrid, Prado   20
Malmö, Museum   150
Milan   137 (Tecnofoto Sella)
Minneapolis, Minneapolis Institute of Art   378
Munich, Bayerische Staatsgemäldesammlungen   60, 67, 346
— Verwaltung der Staatlichen Schlösser, Gärten und Seen   176, 181, 317
New York, Cooper-Hewitt Museum (Scott Hyde)   3, 81, 82, 107, 116, 145, 151, 183, 184, 187, 189, 192, 209, 226, 234, 238, 240, 262, 270, 271, 278, 287, 302, 313, 320, 327, 330, 332, 347, 360, 361, 370, 403
— Metropolitan Museum of Art   9, 43, 58, 68, 84, 97, 119, 120,

This book was printed in August 1982 by
Imprimeries Paul Attinger, Neuchâtel
Photolithographs: CLG Fotolito, Verona (colour plates) and
Atesa Argraf, Geneva (black-and-white plates)
Setting: Photocomposition EP, Lausanne
Binding: Schumacher AG, Schmitten
Designer: Marcel Berger